Inspiring Leadership for Uncertain Times

BY

KARLIN SLOAN

ISBN: 9781087860770

EPUB ISBN: 9781087882871

Table of Contents

Author's Foreword

In light of a massive societal shift happening this March 2020, we've gotten to a new stage of facing change in an era of uncertainty. It's with that in mind that I'm re-releasing this book (formerly UnFear; Facing Change in an Era of Uncertainty), for a new audience, in a new era.

The principles of Inspiring Leadership and the four practices of Alignment are evergreen, and they are of critical importance in challenging times. We need inspiring leadership in these times, to take these four key steps to keep focused on what creates positive impact, ground people in what's important and reduce fear:

- Accept what is, and focus on the future

- Build relationships and community

- View challenges as opportunities

- Practice physical and mental discipline

It is in the most stressful moments that leaders are most important. In a crisis, others look to you for answers, for a calm mind and a strong perspective. They want to hear that they're part of something larger than themselves, that you've got their back, that we're all for one and one for all, and that we will help each other get through the crisis and potentially become stronger for it.

It is in that spirit that I offer you this book, to help you to build your confidence and capability during times of fear and stress. In this time of deep change, it is my privilege to be a support to leaders just like you. To join our virtual community of like minded leaders you can download our app (www.inspiringleadership.io) "Inspiring Leadership" available for Android and in the App store, and I'll see you there.

Karlin Sloan

Introduction

"If we don't change, we'll end up in the direction we're going."

—Chinese proverb

As a leadership development consultant, I have spent my career with people in business, NGOs, government, and not-for-profits who are focused, competent, talented and who have a deep sense of their personal power to impact those around them.

Recently, those same people are having doubts. They doubt their ability to lead their companies through increasingly challenging times. They doubt their ability to protect their loved ones in a world experiencing ecological, health and social crises. And they doubt our collective human family's ability to solve the problems facing us on a global scale.

Our organizations, both large and small, are facing the need to adapt to rapid change that is not predictable or particularly controllable.

If those who lead us are in doubt, then who can we turn to to inspire us, to calm our fears, and to build a path to a better future? How will we effectively address immense changes as individuals, groups, organizations, and as a world community? There is no more important time for inspiring leadership.

Inspiring leaders are those who practice Alignment.

They are leaders who cultivate personal and organizational openness, adaptability, and meaning. They are leaders who practice confidence in our ability to create a positive outcome no matter what the circumstance. They are the ones who will get us there. They are capable of aligning themselves to their higher purpose and inspiration, aligning others to a shared goal, and to aligning resources to get the job done.

Websters Dictionary gives this definition of Alignment: "an arrangement of groups or forces in relation to one another".

Alignment does not mean being fearless in the face of uncertainty. Fearlessness can be reckless and unthinking. Or not taking into account the reality of a given situation or learning from our emotional response to that reality.

Alignment is different. Alignment means confidence in our ability to create a positive future. It is a state of openness, adaptability, and integration. Through Alignment, we can confront reality and create options, innovations, and opportunity. It is the place from which we can suspend our conclusions about outcomes, from which we can grow, change, and build.

Alignment is a state of complete possibility, where we use all we've been given, to actively create the world we wish to inhabit.

Are We in Shock?

Things are changing fast.

We have a constant stream of information that is coming in at all times from all sources. We have technology that is constantly changing and that the workplace is always adapting to. And now? We have a unique pandemic that won't just affect one country or one continent, it is affecting the whole globe. In case it isn't already clear: technology and a powerful global supply chain have made it possible for the globe to come together.

We are shocked into awareness that we are one human family.

We are also shocked into awareness that many of our institutions and organizations are not completely prepared for this reality.

After years of training in organizational change management, my conclusion is that we can't really "manage" the kind of rapid, complex change our world is experiencing right now. Managing has the connotation of taking control, creating a plan, moving pieces forward in a linear progression. But that's simply not possible with the kind of change we are facing.

People who lead and manage are hit with a new level of complexity in decision-making, time management, and simple focus. We can plan, shift, adapt and envision, but we may have more influence than control over many of the situations in which we find ourselves.

In 1970 Alvin Toffler wrote a seminal book on the concept of "future shock". This takes the idea that some change has become too rapid and too complex to deal with from a place of calm and rationality. The results of future shock are like a shock to the body or the nervous system; we are unable to process the information and adapt quickly enough.

Daryl Conner, in his book *Managing at the Speed of Change*, had this incredible example of "future shock":

> Once, after conducting a briefing of our research findings for the White House staff, I was approached by a Pentagon official who told me that one of the ways that they were seeing future shock was in the open revolt of fighter pilots against more technology. The pilots were saying: "Don't put any more technology in the cockpit. I can't keep up with everything, and you're going to kill me". The pilots were not complaining about bad or unwanted technology, it was technology that they had asked for and even helped design. They were simply saying, "My plate is too full now. Don't bring me any more opportunities. I can't digest what I have".

If we are to pay attention to Toffler's wisdom, we have reached the point of extensive "future shock" in our organizations worldwide. The behaviors you may see in your organization as a result of future shock might be irritation, diverted or scattered attention, irrational or scattershot decision-making, decreased risk-taking, defensive and blaming behavior, avoidance of direct communication, and decreased team effectiveness. In light of the Covid-19 pandemic, there is also increased anxiety, depression, and isolating, not just physically but altogether distancing from others.

These change-induced behaviors are increasing—and rapidly.

How can our organizations, whether corporate or not-for-profit, government or local community groups, get out of shock and into collective action? How will we be able to look directly at the pressures we're under and transform ourselves to fit the world that is coming into being? The answer is Alignment.

The Beautiful Truth

The amazing possibility that lies in this incredible time of turmoil is inside each one of us. It is the possibility for true, pure transformation. When we are confronted with chaos and the push to change, we have the option of seeing our world with new eyes. We have the option of asking ourselves questions that can move us to new realities.

We can ask personal questions: Who am I? What am I a part of? What are my gifts and talents? How can I contribute to bringing about the future that I want, rather than passively accepting a future that is handed to me? What kind of leader can I be? What is within me, waiting to be unleashed, that would come forward if I had no fear?

Leaders in organizations of all types now need to ask challenging questions: How will we be viable—presently and in the future? How can we build the kind of workplace and the kind of impact that we want to have? How will our organization contribute to a better world? What is my role in all of this, and what do I need to stand for, to fight for? What are my opportunities to use my strengths and talents to contribute?

Leaders need to be able to envision their organization as part of the interconnected globe, and what kind of questions global interdependence raises and what kind of preparations the organization needs to take. The focus now is on how we impact the whole, and the community of people all through the supply chain that make or farm our ingredients, transport our goods, populate our offices, live near our factories, and buy our products.

The beautiful truth is that organizations worldwide are changing and becoming more focused on the long term and the big picture. Short-term thinking and planning are out!

There will be ambiguity. But now is the time to create tolerance for it. Yes, it can feel like being pulled through a meat grinder, but here's the upside. Assume there will also be opportunities inherent in all of our experiences.

We can turn the lead of present circumstance into the gold of the future.

The beautiful truth is that every day people are waking up to the idea that we can each make a difference, and when we organize ourselves into communities of contribution, we can change the world for the better. We are beginning to align the needs of humanity with the work of our organizations.

Why Do You Need This Book?

You may be looking to develop your own ability to practice Alignment personally or professionally during a crisis, you could be leading an organization or team in turmoil, or it may be that you're looking for a few examples of leaders who have survived and even broken through to great new thinking, through challenging circumstances.

You may be going through change—asking yourself questions about who you are and what you want for the future of your work, your company, and your life. You've come to the right place.

We all go through changes at work; from the moment we're hired into a new role to the first time we have to give someone else performance feedback, we're constantly changing and developing. We also all face normal human challenges like juggling work and family, getting laid off, or even coping with illness and reinventing ourselves. We may survive a crisis, a conflict with our team, be acquired, restructured, downsized, or outsourced.

In this book, we'll explore both organizational and individual Alignment and how you can proactively engage your own capacity to let go of what is blocking you from your best work. We'll look at how to move beyond fear-based behaviors and activate confidence in yourself, your work team, and your organization *no matter what the circumstance.*

Why Do <u>We</u> Need This Book?

Our world is on the brink of enormous change. Natural and man-made disasters are affecting more and more people. Covid-19 is changing the landscape of work and life, and epidemiologists are telling us there will be more like this.

The world population is set to explode from seven billion now to nine billion in 2050. We are consuming resources at six times the rate of what we can regenerate. Oil prices are plunging to negative numbers, climate change is barreling toward us with unthinkable consequences. Food riots have begun around the world because of global shortages in staple crops and fear of supply chain disruption is everywhere. Forty percent of land-based species are threatened within thirty to fifty years, depending upon whom you listen to. Artificial Intelligence is evolving at a pace many of us cannot comprehend—and the changes to our society and our world will be enormous. Many of us are increasingly disconnected from our local communities, not knowing our neighbors and lacking a sense of social cohesion and shared experience.

There is no time to lose!

Importantly, we need the tools and capacities to get out of fright, flight, and paralysis, and to use fear wisely and consciously to inform our decisions rather than to make our decisions for us.

Our world needs us to come together with a new view of possibility, with openness and creativity, and with the will to change—not just to adapt to what is, but to create what might be.

It is time for us to become globally aware.

It is time to acknowledge the tremendous challenges that we are faced with as a human civilization, and to see the opportunities inherent in our individual and organizational lives to improve our collective circumstances. We need to recognize the great gifts we've been given—our own glorious, unique attributes and abilities that the world needs now—and we need to give those gifts to the world. There is no time like the present, and no one better positioned to transform yourself and the world than you.

In this book, we'll explore inspiring leadership and cultivating both organizational and individual Alignment. We'll focus on how you can proactively engage your own capacity to let go of what is blocking you from your best work. And we'll address the new standards required for leadership; leaders who have the ability to look at the big societal picture, focus on ethics and values, know that our actions have a powerful impact, and strive for that impact to be positive and exponential.

Chapter 1

From Fear to Alignment

"So, first of all, let me assert my firm belief that the only thing we have to fear is fear itself".

—Franklin D Roosevelt

When we operate in a state of fear, we shut down our best thinking and instead we operate from reactivity to immediate danger. If we stay in that state of fear, we are consistently training our brains *out* of our best thinking.

Think about your work environment.

Is it a place where people are concerned for their jobs? Are they uncomfortable with or distrustful of feedback? Is there a consistent background state of anxiety? OR, is it a place you are excited to go to, where new ideas are cultivated, where there is a sense of possibility and promise, and where you are unafraid to express yourself, to ask questions, or to come up with new ways of working?

Most of our organizations are a bit of both. During times of stress and challenge—and dare I say future shock—they can shift quickly toward fear based behavior and decisions. Fight, flight, and freeze are the hard-wired responses to fear that stop us from making good decisions and acting from the best part of ourselves. They are also what get organizations into trouble.

Remember, Alignment is confidence in our ability to create a positive outcome no matter what the circumstance, and it means getting ourselves out of survival mode.

You may remember from your Psychology 101 class the idea of Abraham Maslow's hierarchy of needs[1]. It's pretty simple: The hierarchy starts at the

---

[1] A.H. Maslow, "A Theory of Human Motivation", *Psychological Review* 50(4) (1943): 370-96

bottom with survival. If we don't have food, water and our other physical survival needs met, that becomes our complete focus.

As we move up the ladder, and we have shelter covered, we get to more sophisticated needs. We move to getting our emotional needs met through love and connection to others. Beyond that, we have the basic human need for respect—from others and from ourselves (self-esteem). At the top of the pyramid are two more areas. One is self-actualization. This is described by Maslow's student, Dr. Wayne Dyer, as "to be free of the good opinion of others" and "to do things not simply for the outcomes but because it's the reason you are here on earth".[2] Self-actualization is the point at which we connect to purpose and meaning beyond our own physical and emotional needs.

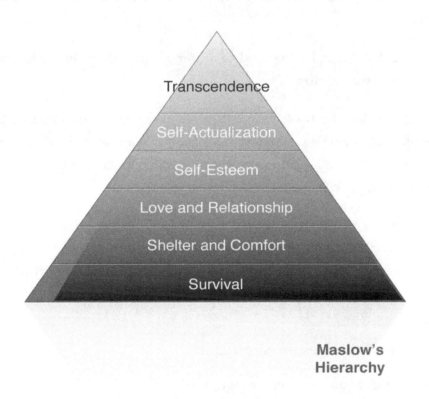

Maslow's Hierarchy

---

[2] Hay House's "I Can Do It!" 2009 conference in Tampa, Florida, released in theaters as *Wishes Fulfilled*

The final category was created at the end of Maslow's life, and that category is one he felt had been missing: transcendence. When we transcend, we give back to the world without the need for our own gain.

Why is this model useful when we look to create Alignment in our organizations? Because so many of us *revert* to survival-level behaviors in the face of fear, even when, in the moment, those needs are covered. When we are worried about survival, we don't have the capacity to align with higher-level behaviors like searching for meaning, giving to others, and contributing our gifts and talents in a positive way. Instead, we become self-focused and fearful.

To create Alignment, leaders need to help move people up the ladder from the basics to the very top.

If you're reading this book, chances are you have your survival needs taken care of. That doesn't mean you don't *feel* like you're in survival mode. These sometimes-unconscious responses to our outside environment can shape our behavior, our beliefs, and our outcomes in unhelpful ways.

Fear is useful when you're at that bottom level of the Maslow pyramid. Without fear, we couldn't survive. We need to be able to activate that fight or flight instinct in times of immediate physical danger. It's not as useful when we are beyond that immediate moment of life-or-death peril.

The Four Practices of Alignment

Fear of the future, fear of change, fear of the unknown and fear of overwhelm—what are we to do with these increasing fears?

Alignment practices allow leaders to interact with a rapidly changing environment successfully.

We need to bring out our amazing human capacity to be thoughtful and conscious before we act; we must cultivate our ability to operate from a state of Alignment. Leaders who succeed in an environment of rapid change use the four practices that create that Alignment:

- Accept what is, and focus on the future

- Build relationships and community

- View challenges as opportunities

- Practice physical and mental discipline

As you read the stories of leaders and their organizations overcoming obstacles, dealing with tough times, managing growth or expansion, coming out of a bad situation, or discovering exciting new ways to do things, you'll see these same four practices over and over again.

One of my favorite examples of Alignment, in the face of seemingly unending adversity, is in the leadership of Ernest Shackleton. In December of 1914, Shackleton and his crew set out on the ship, *Endurance*, to Antarctica; one of the last frontiers of the golden age of exploration. One month later, his ship was frozen in pack ice, never to sail again.

Known to his men as "the boss," Shackleton quickly engaged the men in constant activities, both work and play, as they camped on the ice, waiting for the coming thaw. He encouraged unity in his team and made everyone equal by removing all rank. And he gave them a new, shared mission: keeping every man alive.

The men of the *Endurance* were buoyed by Shackleton, who kept a focus on the future and looked for solutions at every turn. When the thaw came and the ice began to break up, the crew set out in three lifeboats to find dry land. After five days at sea in temperatures of minus twenty degrees Fahrenheit (-30°C), they reached Elephant Island, a desolate place inhabited by penguins. It was soon clear that there was no chance of rescue.

The crew patched together one lifeboat, and Shackleton and five other men set out across the roughest ocean in the world to make it to South Georgia Island. For three days they walked, despite deep hunger and exhaustion, to reach the whaling station. Sea ice stopped Shackleton from rescuing his men, immediately. When he finally reached Elephant Island with a tug four months later, he rescued every single member of the Endurance crew[3].

Shackleton's ability to accept the real, focus on the positive future, build relationships and community, and view challenges as opportunities enabled his crew to survive. He understood the circumstances they were in but he never gave in to believing in a terrible future. He kept the faith, and helped his crew to develop constant physical and mental discipline that helped them stay alive no matter what happened.

Just as Shackleton led his team through difficult circumstances, our business leaders today face enormous challenge and unprecedented change, and when we're in charge it's up to us to keep ourselves and our teams rallied to meet whatever lies before us.

How do we develop these marvelous abilities required for Alignment? We must reorient ourselves to developing our strengths and to seeing possibilities in what's before us, no matter how difficult.

The Strengths Revolution

There is a revolution happening in our organizations, and it is a revolution of strengths. Voices like those of Martin Seligman, Marcus Buckingham, David Cooperrider, Diana Whitney, Fred Luthans, and Kim Cameron are publicly declaring a new worldview in organizational life. I am proud to say my organization has been a part of that strengths revolution for the last twenty years, and that every day that we help another leader to engage their best thinking, make clear decisions, communicate effectively, build their

---

[3] Carline Alexander, *The Endurance: Shackleton's Legendary Antarctic Expedition*, Knopf, 1998

team's capacity, or get out of reactive, fear-based behavior, I am satisfied we are helping to bring about the possibility of a positive future.

The strengths revolution is not about a "Pollyanna" worldview that looks only at the positive to the exclusion of all else; it is the development of a new balance. We are naturally trained to use our "critical eye" to view what's ahead. We are naturally trained to use our critical thinking and skills of discernment to find and solve problems. Our ability to find and solve problems is a great asset, but it can't be the only tool in our tool box.

To address an intense barrage of change and complexity, we need a new dose of optimism and commitment to searching for and building the good. That perspective, that "appreciative eye," is critical for our finding new possibilities and building new options, new futures. To appreciate means to recognize the worth of something, to understand it, or to broaden and build value. That's just what we need to cultivate right now.

What we focus on broadens and builds, and when we focus on weaknesses and threats without focusing equally on strengths and opportunities, we go out of balance and start amplifying our reactivity to fear. The organizations that fail are often those that stay reactive and fearful of change, be it from market conditions, competition, or a fragmented and disengaged workforce.

The best and most exciting organizations are those that focus on creating a positive future and work toward that future. They engage both the minds and hearts of their employees because there is a shared sense of achievement and a promise of creating something positive together.

The four qualities of Alignment provide us with a much-needed formula to help us step away from future shock and back into strength and empowerment in the face of change.

How do you know if you're living in a state of fear versus Alignment?

Fear Versus Alignment - Lawrence's Story

Lawrence, an operations executive in a large consumer products company, had been letting fear get the best of him for six months. He had just returned from a long stint in South America as the head of a division and he was having trouble integrating back into U.S. culture.

14

He had led his team well and he had been very popular in Brazil. Unfortunately, in the U.S., Lawrence had alienated some of the senior management team by not communicating enough, not paying attention to politics, and not aligning himself with anyone above him. He was told there wasn't a permanent role for him in the U.S. organization after his assignment was complete, and he was asked to wait and take on a role doing "special projects" for the COO.

Lawrence felt slighted being relegated to special projects. He started working on an audit of facilities in the regions, but he said no to running a large technology implementation because it was housed in the HR function, and he felt that the power players in the organization wouldn't see his value if he worked with HR. He asked to be considered for another position in Latin America or Europe.

In the meantime, Lawrence's self-criticism grew. He second-guessed himself. He started behaving erratically, snapping at his co-workers, and criticizing his successor in Brazil. Laurence's internal condemnation was at an all-time high when we met for the first time. "I've ruined my career," Lawrence said. "If I lose this job, I'll lose my family."

Whoa! That's quite a leap!

Lawrence's fear had done a number on him. It was sabotaging his success by attacking his very belief in himself, causing him to come up with disastrous assumptions about his future. At home, his wife was terrified that Lawrence was going to lose his job and angry that he wasn't focusing on his two young children more. At work, his boss was disappointed in Lawrence's lack of engagement and concerned that he wasn't being a team player. What a setup for failure!

There are two ways we can deal with fear.

We can let fear (either conscious or unconscious) drive our behavior reactively. When we are reactive instead of thoughtful we respond impulsively without thinking about the outcome we want.

What about responding from Alignment? That would require us to understand fear for its value. Fear's aim is survival! In a situation of physical life and death, fear can move us out of the way of a falling object, get us to run from a hungry animal or alert our body to gear up to fight when we need to defend ourselves. All fears are operating for a reason. Fear possesses positive intent.

In business, our instantaneous responses to fear are not usually that useful. In fact, fight, flight, and paralysis are often the worst ways to react to work situations and can get in the way of all of our best thinking and action.

Lawrence had gotten himself into a fear-based trap. We developed a new goal: for Lawrence to act from a new state...a state of Alignment.

Lawrence opted to look at the past analytically in order to learn from it, and to face the future with a sense of possibility. He came up with a proposal for a new special research project to determine if there was an opportunity in an emerging market in Latin America. He made the case that his extensive experience in Brazil would mean greater awareness of cultural issues. He was proactive, positive, and when he spoke with the COO he advocated for himself, and for the opportunity he saw in this new role.

Fear Versus Alignment in Organizational Leadership - Robert's Story

Robert is an inspiring entrepreneurial leader with a small advertising firm based in California. When Covid-19 hit the USA his small team was frightened, concerned for the wellbeing of their families, distracted and completely unfocused as they shifted to working virtually versus in person.

One very popular team member had been let go, and Robert had taken on extra hours, as had three others on the team who were attempting to do more with less.

He started to notice that when the team came together for weekly meetings, instead of being their normal lively and challenging selves, they were completely silent, waiting for him to speak and tell them what was next. They were afraid of more layoffs, of losing their jobs, and of asking for support or assistance to get the job done.

As a leader, what was Robert to do with this? They were too fearful to talk openly about any problems they were having, and he was sure they would not meet their targets for the quarter. When he challenged them, or confronted their fearful behavior, he got a wall of stony silence. No one would risk the honesty required to tell him that they were in deep trouble.

Does this situation sound familiar?

Robert shifted the time he spent on outreach to the team and created two touch points per day for every person. One was a 30 minute one-on-one on the phone. The other was a team meeting for one hour per day on zoom. Each Friday they would open a zoom room for the whole day, and people could talk to each other as needed. If someone was busy, they shut down their video/audio temporarily, then opened back up for shared "office hours".

That level of connection was what it took to get everyone focused.

Robert's strategy for navigating this new business landscape needed to change. Instead of meeting quarterly revenue goals, the new goal was to retain every customer for the future. He gave the team the assignment to connect with every single customer and offer something free to assist them through this time.

The team was also asked to spend one team meeting brainstorming options for cost-cutting and moving through the next six months with the goal of breaking even versus increasing profitability.

This shift was messaged by Robert every day. Repetition of the same message was important in order for everyone to really hear what the priority was. The team started focusing on the new goal of building relationships that would last versus booking new business.

While Robert is still in the middle of this shift, his team is excited to get to work, to focus, to stay connected to each other and to their clients.

In organizations, fear can shut down the productivity and effectiveness of a team, fast. We stop thinking clearly and start operating based on faulty assumptions. We forget the incredible interconnections and interdependence in our global economy and in our environment. We miss important details and scramble to get things done rather than thinking.

Which Organizations Will Succeed?

Organizations that are agile, meaning-filled and contribute to our interdependent systems will succeed because they practice Alignment. They will be sustainable, flexible, and will have new ways of working from strengths. They will not focus just on the levels of survival and comfort; they will be organizations of self-actualization and transcendence. They will activate a sense of purpose in their employees and their customers.

BBMG, a branding and integrated marketing agency in New York and San Francisco, conducted a major study in partnership with Global Strategy Group and Bagatto. The report combines ethnographic research in three U.S. markets with a national survey of two thousand and seven adults. Results showed that nearly nine in ten Americans say the words "conscious consumer" describe them, and that they are more likely to buy from companies that manufacture energy-efficient products (90 percent), support fair labor and trade practices (87 percent), promote health and safety benefits (88 percent), and commit to environmentally friendly practices (87 percent) if products are of equal price and quality.[4]

---

[4] Raphael Bemporad and Mitch Baranowski, *Conscious Consumers Are Changing the Rules of Marketing. Are You Ready?* November 2007

18

Companies that practice alignment understand that consumers are changing, employees are changing, and consciousness is changing.

There are large, traditional organizations that have never stopped connecting their employees to values. Their focus on meaning means they attract and retain the best and brightest. Then there's a whole new breed of organizations and brands out there, and they want to make the world better for their customers, their employees, and everyone else! They have a sense of purpose—and it's unstoppable.

Liberty Mutual's Creed

Founded in 1912, Liberty Mutual is no whippersnapper of a company. When walking into the lobby of the building, you are greeted with an enormous wall that showcases Liberty Mutual's creed:

> We are engaged in a great mutual enterprise. It is great because it seeks to prevent crippling injuries and death by removing the causes of home, highway, and work accidents. It is great because it deals in the relief of pain and sorrow and fear and loss. It is great because it works to preserve and protect the things people earn and build and own and cherish. Its true greatness will be measured by our power to help people live safer, more secure lives.

Just having the visceral experience of that creed on the wall makes an impact on employees, vendors, and customers who walk into their Boston offices. Their commitment to a larger purpose has helped them focus on safety breakthroughs and innovative programs that have helped to reduce workplace injury, illness, and disability.

Nearly 100 years later, they continue to be serious about their values, which impacts both employees and customers. Their commitment to philanthropy goes beyond their foundation, giving in excess of $52 million in 2018, and extends to thousands of Liberty Mutual employees engaging in community service of all kinds, all helping people to live safer, more secure lives. They volunteer at food banks, serve on boards, build homes—and their organization helps them to feel great about that contribution by measuring and sharing their great work in their annual report.

TOMS Impact

TOMS is an innovative company created by Blake Mycoskie and focused on providing shoes, eyewear and bags not just to their customers, but shoes for impoverished children, sight restoration, and birthkits for safe deliveries. On their website, there is no "company story"; instead, it's "your impact". Customers can feel fantastic about their contribution to the world by spending money on TOMS products. Since May 2006, Tom's has given over 100 million shoes to children who need them, 780,000 sight restorations and 722,000 weeks of safe water.

GreenSole Shoes Re-Use

Speaking of shoes...GreenSole shoes is an Indian company with a similar mission of delivering shoes to the underprivileged. So far GreenSole has provided over 150,000 pairs of shoes, saved 5,500,000 lbs of CO_2 emissions, saved shoes from landfills and have prevented disease in the process.

> As athletes, Shriyans Bhandari and Ramesh Dhami ran hundreds of kilometers every year. They also ran through at least three to four pairs of sport shoes every year. The soles were in good condition but the shoe sides tore within months. The duo always wondered if they could find some use for the intact soles of these quality sport shoes. A bit of research led to the idea of refurbishing them into trendy slippers. That brainwave eventually spawned an eco-friendly enterprise that reuses shoe soles and is appropriately named GreenSole. - Hindu Business Line

Worldwide every year more than 350,000,000 pairs of shoes are discarded, while as per the recent report by the UN World Health Oorganization, 1.5 billion people are infected by diseases that could be prevented by wearing proper footwear. Check them out online and see if you can do a "shoe drive" to donate your used shoes and repurpose them for something great.

Banco Sol's Poverty Alleviation through Microfinancing

Pancho Otero knew in 1991, when he began running the world's largest commercially viable micro-lending institution in Latin America, that there was a great opportunity to build wealth in Bolivia, and not the traditional way. Seventy percent of Bolivian citizens live below the poverty line. He knew that he could help people help themselves through microcredit. Knowing he didn't want to create something that was modeled on a traditional philanthropic model, Otero saw the opportunity to build wealth for his investors while building wealth in the poorest sectors of developing countries. He saw the opportunity for Alignment.

In early 2010, I had the privilege of sitting down with Pancho Otero and asking him about his pioneering story:

> "My boss, Fernando Romero invented several financial vehicles and tools. He said, "This is a bank. It has to serve the community". He also said drop all this wording about the poor. Drop the fear that the poor won't pay it back. This is about entrepreneurs. The operations are very small. They have markets and suppliers. It's on a smaller scale. There are cultural differences, but the concepts are the same. Subsistence people are great business people—they need to make it work.
>
> I learned from the peasants. An American NGO came to work with us. Someone knew some Bolivian investors and convinced them to do urban microfinance. We had a board of sophisticated finance people—capital markets types. It didn't take them long to say, "You've got tellers, security guards…this is a bank!" This

model is about taking money from our country and having it go back into our country.

We invented the Bolivian model. We go where we're invited. We look for a group to come up with a couple hundred thousand dollars. We see it as a start-up. We operate there for about a year until we reach equilibrium—it pays for itself. We make sure that local investors understand that these "poor people" pay their loans punctually, that they have legitimate businesses, that they know how to invest well, that the loans have tremendous impact.

We sometimes bring in a central bank; we have to look at the local laws before we go commercial in a big way. Usury laws may need to be changed. After we do this for a year and have enough people looking at it, we put together a bank or finance company. We bring in directors from that community. The reason these people don't have access to credit is because they don't have traditional guarantees or collateral. It's true, you can't lend without a guarantee. It sounds like a gift. The loan has to be credible.

We did groups. We said as a group, if he can't pay, all of you have to pay for him. This group guarantee system requires you to really believe in and support the members of the community. If you ask these people to make this enormous commitment, this enormous effort, the staff must show they are capable of enormous commitment and effort as well. They become teams; they put their personal interest aside. We call the bank staff a solidarity group—a group of amigos. The group becomes very cohesive, very participatory. Nobody wins unless everybody wins."

Banco Sol went onto become the first microfinance institution in history to issue dividends to shareholders. The bank declared cash dividends of forty-five cents per share on 1996 earnings of $1.1 million. Banco Sol boasts better profitability rates than some of the world's biggest banks. It serves eighty thousand clients with loans averaging eight hundred dollars (U.S.) and a recovery rate of 99 percent.

When we break out of the antiquated idea that successful organizations are the ones that are ruthlessly pursuing the bottom line with no regard for the health of our world, we break out of the destructive model of short term- ism and fear that holds us back from making our world a better place. So how do we get there? How do we inspire Alignment in ourselves and our organizations? First, we need to accept the real and focus on the future. And reality is not always pretty.

Chapter 2

How Bad Things May Be Good

"Character cannot be developed in ease and quiet. Only through experience of trial and suffering can the soul be strengthened, ambition inspired, and success achieved."

—Helen Keller

I'm going to tell you something you already know: **Bad things happen.**

Accepting those bad things, and moving forward, is the first practice of Alignment. Whether developing individual, team, or organizational Alignment, we all need to remember why seemingly negative events can have positive results. They may not be positive in the short term, or positive for us on a personal level, but here are a few arguments for why we may want to look at negatives as opportunities.

Creative Destruction

Sometimes we need to clear away the old to make way for the new. When your division is cut loose, your entrepreneurial venture crumbles, or your personal life splits in two with a divorce, loss, or disruption, it is tough to remember that as long as you exist, there will be a new day ahead. There is a natural cycle of life that includes death.

The adaptive cycle model, taken from the realm of ecology, is a tool to think about resilience in systems. It looks at how systems grow, change, adapt, or die out. It was developed by looking at a comparative study of ecosystems. C.S. Holling, a proponent of adaptive cycle thinking, says, "The bewildering, entrancing, unpredictable character of the natural world and people, the richness, diversity and changeability of life, come from that evolutionary dance generated by cycles of growth, collapse, reorganization, renewal and re-establishment".

Four distinct phases have been identified within the adaptive cycle:

1. growth or exploitation

2. conservation

3. collapse or release

4. reorganization

The best example to illustrate the adaptive cycle is a forest fire. Things fall apart—creative destruction. Things are reduced to simpler elements. Then you have release—the biomass is released. You get a fertile landscape where organisms find the new, free energy. It's highly competitive for the organisms that come in and try to use that energy to grow, and nothing can build up biomass at first because of the massive competition. Eventually you get a die-out and a reorganization into a lesser level of diversity.

What this particular resilience theory argues is that we must be able to go through all these cycles in any system, whether an ecosystem or an organization. In protecting forests, for example, we've moved from the idea of stopping all fires to realizing that healthy ecosystems may need small fires to clear away, to make the forest more resilient over time.

This resilience theory is also useful in organizational life. An idea is born then developed into products or services. Resources are diverted into launching the product. It is healthy to have parts of an organization collapse in order to release those resources for other things.

In business today, we see an argument about the adaptive cycle playing out with the would-be collapse of the cruise ship industry. Should those resources—that human and intellectual capital—be released and used toward a new, more viable enterprise? When you're on the losing end of a layoff or a failed business enterprise, it's hard to remember that it's part of a natural cycle of death and rebirth and that there may be a positive reason behind that failure. Not to pick on the cruise industry, but April 2020 is not the best moment to be on a cruise ship either as a passenger or a crew member. Take it from nature and remember that your energy doesn't disappear; it needs to be channelled into a new, more productive direction.

We tend to look at our companies as if they are machines. If we start looking at our organizations as if they were living, breathing systems that are participating in a healthy cycle, it makes a powerful difference in how we manage and see the organism we're part of. Healthy organisms, healthy systems, have an immune response to what stresses their system. They also have a natural end point, a death, when the matter they are made out of changes into something different.

The Human Response to Pain Is Creativity

After a collapse or release there is reorganization.

We have an incredible capacity to prevail despite terrible odds. We are, sometimes despite ourselves, incredibly adaptive creatures. We have created technologies that allow us with our vulnerable human bodies to survive in almost any environment on earth, including deep in the oceans and even in space. It is often because of suffering or challenge that we take actions and attempt to make things better. Without the darkness, there can be no light.

Many artists, inventors, innovators, and thinkers talk about their best work evolving as a way to cope with pain or suffering. That work is a gift to the world. The French artist Henri Matisse created some of his most beautiful and well-known works after he was diagnosed with cancer and underwent a difficult surgery. Bedridden, or wheelchair bound, he worked with assistants to create cut paper collages that comprised his book, *Jazz*. He said, "Only what I created after the illness constitutes my real self: free, liberated".[5] There is great opportunity when there's tough work to be done.

LifeStraw is the Give Back program for the Verstergaard company, and it's an example of creativity and innovation in response to human pain. The

_____

[5] http://www.henri-matisse.net/cut_outs.html

LifeStraw costs only a few dollars and provides a year of safe water consumption for people in need. A simple, single sealed unit design with no need for electricity or moving parts enables this device to be used anywhere people need to take a drink, protecting people from disease and bacteria. Rather than despairing over seemingly insurmountable challenges, we have the capacity to innovate and create solutions to pain and suffering, providing positive impact in the world.

The Dark Night of the Soul and the Birth of Compassion

Most of us experience a dark night of the soul when we have a loss — a moment when we awaken to the fact that life is unfair, that horrors happen to good people, and that we are not in control. It is through our suffering that we can understand the suffering of others, that we can develop compassion for our fellow human beings. Think of the worst things we have on our planet caused by humans: war, injustice, genocide, the worst of human suffering. How is it we make meaning of those things?

When we truly understand the reality that all bad behavior, all horrible deeds committed by people, come from fear, pain, or ignorance, we can have compassion not just for victims, but for those who victimize others. Through that compassion, we are able to transcend our reactivity to pain and suffering, and think before we act. It enables us to stop our own compulsions to violence or negativity in thought or action. Think of a world in which we are all aware of the suffering of others, and feel genuine care and compassion for all beings.

Anya Cordell's mother told her a story that when she was born, she kicked and fussed so much that the doctor "messed up" when he was cutting the umbilical cord and she would always have a "disfigured" navel.

> My journey included my teen years, when my deepest yearning was to be a supermodel, to the time when I realized that the beauty-obsessed culture was oppressive (and that I was oppressing myself more cruelly than anyone), to when I finally

made the connection that any hatred of natural appearance was a terrible injustice which leads to untold suffering and destruction.

Anya suffered from painful body image issues, but out of her pain she became aware that she was not alone, that we all live our lives from inside a body, and that we are all subject to what she calls "appearance-ism".

As a writer, speaker, and teacher, she was asked to present her book *Race: An Open and Shut Case* in South Africa, at the parliament of world religions. As she was preparing to leave on the trip, a black neighbor of hers was murdered in a vicious attack by a white supremacist group. This motivated her further to help the world understand racism, stereotyping, and appearance bias.

After September 11, violence in the U.S. increased 1,700 percent, according to Human Rights Watch. Anya says, "Innocent Arabs, Muslims, Sikhs, Hindus, South Asians and others, most of whom were U.S. citizens, were victims of self-avowed 'patriots' who, unable to kill Osama bin Laden, settled for the guy behind the counter at their local gas station". Her own personal story, her personal understanding of what it feels like to be different and to have been judged—by self and other—based on looks has informed a life of compassion and care.

> Not only has this journey led me to reclaim myself, it has led me to incredible people, experiences, and relationships. It has enabled me to feel that, to some extent, I am part of the solution to a violent, polarized world. It is much more gratifying to work to change the world, instead of pouring my resources into changing my own appearance.[6]

---

6 www.anyacordell.com

The Existing System Cannot Hold

"The GDP as it's contrived right now is really a system where we are stealing from the future, selling it in the present, and we're calling it GDP."

—Paul Hawken

When something breaks apart, it is possible that it was not a healthy system to begin with, or that it's reached the end of its natural lifecycle. When a company fails, or when an economy crashes, it may not have been sustainable in the first place.

Let's start with the basics of un-sustainability. Here's a true story:

During World War II, a small island off the coast of Alaska in the Bering Strait was home to a U.S. Coast Guard monitoring station. Nineteen men were stationed there and, as a backup food source, the U.S. government supplied them with a group of twenty-nine reindeer. The men and the reindeer lived peacefully on the island until the end of the war, and not a single reindeer was sacrificed for food. The men left and the reindeer stayed.

St. Matthew Island provided a treasure trove of food in the form of four-inch-thick mats of lichen for the reindeer and, as there were no natural predators, their numbers started to swell. In 1957, Dave Klein, a biologist with the Fish and Wildlife Service, visited the island and found a thriving population of fat and happy reindeer: one thousand three hundred and fifty in all.

In 1963, Klein returned to the island to find a disturbing reality. Six thousand reindeer had nearly taken over the tiny island. You may guess what happened next. Klein returned to the island in 1966 and found only destruction. Much of the vegetation of the small island had been eaten by a population un-culled by natural predators, and there were only forty-two living reindeer left. Skeletons littered the island and only one male survived, with abnormal antlers, probably unable to reproduce. [7]

What happens when a system is unsustainable? Talk about acknowledging the real. This is reality, and it's no joke.

Steady exponential growth in consumption is no longer possible because we have reached the point at which we are using our natural resources faster than we can replace them. There was a study done by Harvard University and the Nature Conservancy in 2007 about the impact of urban growth on ecosystems. They found that the scale of resource consumption on earth in 2007 was the equivalent of building a city the size of Vancouver every week.[9] So think about that: using that much steel, concrete, water, oil, and manpower each week. How many weeks will it take for us to run out of some of our most precious resources if we don't think differently? Here's the good news...

7 Ned Rozell, "St. Matthew Island – Overshoot and Collapse." Alaska Science, November 23, 2003 9 "Global Impact of Urbanization Threatening World's Biodiversity and Natural Resources." ScienceDaily. Retrieved January 24, 2010, from http://www.sciencedaily.com/releases/2008/06/080610182856.htm

The System Corrects Itself

Just as the adaptive cycle helps to keep a forest ecosystem healthy, every system has its innate mechanisms that preserve health. Of course, preserving the health of the whole system may require the die-off of parts of that system.

Do not get me wrong. I am not saying that loss isn't painful...but crises give us a chance to rethink how we wish to rebuild the future. It is an opportunity to see how we can do things differently, more ethically, more sustainably and more humanely. It's an opportunity for us to build something new and powerful.

What about changing and moving to Alignment in a crisis? Who will succeed individually and collectively? How can Alignment make our systems more viable in a new era?

We need to start asking the right questions – specifically:

- What do we want our world to look like in the future?

- What structures would enable that world to come into existence?

If we don't want the earth's system to boot our species out, we need to rethink some things.

If we look at Covid-19 as a systemic challenge we need to meet and correct in order to survive; we need to make sure we think strategically. Dr. David Katz wrote a controversial op-ed in the *New York Times* about an approach to herd immunity that was not black and white. He had this to say about the opportunity to shift the dialog to public health versus just illness:

> "First of all, I just want people to understand I'm a physician, I do public health, I trained in epidemiology. It really still looks to me that... 99% of the cases are mild. Most people don't seem to know they have it. A small portion of the cases are severe. The

severe cases occur in people who are old and sick. Sadly, in America there are a lot of young people with type 2 diabetes, hypertension, those are diseases of lifestyle.... here's the interesting bit. The stuff we can't sell to people – eat well, exercise, don't smoke, don't drink excessively, get enough sleep, manage your stress – such potent medicine – we can't sell it because the timeline for harm is too long. Essentially heart disease stalks you in slow motion, type 2 diabetes stalks you in slow motion. And our DNA is wired to fight or flight. You know if it's not coming at me in minutes or days I'm sort of blind to it. Well, Covid-19 is coming at you in minutes and days and everybody is alarmed and all the same things are risk factors. So essentially, this pandemic has turned America's chronic health liabilities into an acute threat. *And there is an opportunity in this crisis...*The very things we're always telling people to do to promote your long term health actually do fortify your immunity against this virus....I would have a national health promotion campaign as part of what we do in an organized way."[8]

Investor Alignment in the Wake of the Madoff Scandal

On an individual level, Lynn Twist, award-winning author of The Soul of Money, spoke with me recently about her work with investors duped by Bernie Madoff's infamous Ponzi scheme. In witnessing them developing their own Alignment, she has seen them shift from calling themselves the Madoff "victims" to "survivors". Lynn speaks about Alignment in the wake of that scandal:

> There's a group, three hundred and fifty families, who found each other on the web and formed a community, and, for a while, they called themselves the Madoff Victims and then they

---

[8] HBO, Real Time with Bill Maher April 24, 2020

changed their name to Madoff Survivors right around the time some of them read, *The Soul of Money* book.

When they were the Madoff Victims—they were angry. They were resentful. They wanted to boil Bernard Madoff in oil—they were just full of rage. When they changed their name, they became focused on getting through the crisis rather than blaming and pointing fingers and being angry.

The group ranges from one family that lost two hundred and eighty-five million dollars (he was an investment banker and a lawyer), to a teacher in Brooklyn, a spinster, who taught sixth grade for 46 years. By the time she retired, all of her living relatives were gone and she had a wonderful retirement package with the State of New York. Then, she got a tip from a friend that she could move all of her money from her IRA into the hands of Bernard Madoff and, of course, she lost everything. She never really had piles of money, but she had enough to live on. Now it's all gone. These people formed a group to support one another.

They're looking at who they were being that created this kind of an outcome in their life, not blaming [Madoff], but really looking at what kind of an economy we're living in that would foster that kind of a scam that would lose sixty-five billion dollars for people who cared about their future. They're looking at what is the money system. What is the SEC doing or not doing that would allow something like that to happen. They're bartering with each other. They're creating and looking at an alternative currency that they would use among each other. The teacher from Brooklyn, she is tutoring the children of the millionaire that he's pulled out of private school, and he has enough cash to pay her rent so she can stay in her apartment. They're just helping each other and they're looking at how they, as a group, are probably the forerunners of what may happen to many, many, many of the rest of us eventually.

If I could ask everyone one question, it would be: "How [are you] using resources—financial and natural resources—that are inconsistent with a sustainable future for all forms of life?" **And if you start reallocating your financial resources away from the old economy and into the new one, what could happen? The death of the old structures and systems that no longer serve us while we midwife the birth of those that do.**

We need to ask the question, "How is this dollar or these ten or these fifty that I'm about to spend…how does it prop up the old economy and can I reallocate it in a way that will foster, foment, and nurture a new economy?"

Think about a green economy, a clean economy, one that's fair, equitable, and healthy for all. And if we ask that question every day, every minute, every hour, we will change our behavior. We'll change the way we think, the way we buy, the way we live, and the way we relate to one another and the planet.[9]

Lynn Twist also says "it's about transformation, and transformation is different than change". Transformation honors and respects the past. It doesn't deny it. It accepts and addresses the past, and transforms it into that which is useful for the future. We need to recognize that the answers we're looking for are found in community, are found in local growing economies right where we live and that our true security is not the accumulation of money in our bank account, but our real security is in our relationship with one another and that's how we will get through, together.

If we take the time to reflect on our own stories of when we have been in Alignment, we can remember that these attributes are in all of us. It is high

---

9   Interview with Lynn Twist, Voice America Radio, World Changers Radio with Karlin Sloan, 2009

time we took stock of those positive ways of coping that we can extract from within ourselves and apply to the rapid, and sometimes uncomfortable, situations we find ourselves in.

Times of deep change confront our very belief systems. Those of us who have benefitted from the materialism of this time have the opportunity to find something meaningful to drive our thinking and our behavior. Think about this quote:

> "The welfare of any segment of humanity is inextricably bound up with the welfare of the whole. Humanity's collective life suffers when any one group thinks of its own well-being in isolation from that of its neighbors or pursues economic gain without regard for how the natural environment, which provides sustenance for all, is affected. A stubborn obstruction, then, stands in the way of meaningful social progress: time and again, avarice and self-interest prevail at the expense of the common good.[10]"

What beliefs do we need to examine right now that will help us move forward in a positive way? We are being made aware right now of how our systems do or do not serve the needs of our collective human species.

We have to focus our energies on ways of living and working that respect ourselves and our earthly home. We have to cultivate our own Alignment and that of our organizations during times of crisis. The next few chapters will show you how.

---

[10] Letter from the Universal House of Justice, March 2017

Chapter 3

Crisis Leadership: What the CEO Needs to Know

"I think the hardest thing about my job is the way Whole Foods Market views itself philosophically...that we are a business dedicated to meeting all the various stakeholders of the company's best interests. And by stakeholders we mean customers, team members, stockholders, community, and the environment...as the CEO, I have to balance the various interests of the different constituencies and stakeholders to create win-win-win scenarios, and that can sometimes be very difficult to do. Everybody wants something from the CEO."

—John Mackey

The job of senior leadership changes when times are tough. No one knows this better than the CEO, founder, president, director—the one who holds the ultimate responsibility for the success, or failure, of an organization. So how can they cultivate organizational resilience? How can they lead with Alignment? How do the four practices relate to being at the top and making the big decisions? This chapter will lead us through the elements of the four steps that senior management needs to take when there is a crisis.

Acknowledge the real and focus on the future.

- Acknowledge harsh realities.

- Move fluidly from short to long-term thinking.

Build relationships and community.

- Inspire others to think bigger and to connect to team identity.

- Develop soft power.

- Measure and build employee engagement.

View challenges as opportunities.

- Drive innovation.

- Conduct a resilience audit.

Practice physical and mental discipline.

- Reorient to the positive core and purpose of the organization.

- Preserve your own optimism and energy for the task at hand.

Acknowledge the Harsh Realities of Your Role

Remember what Shackleton did? He was able to look at the reality of the situation and move forward with a new vision. Recognize the truth of your situation, from an economic perspective as well as an environmental one.

Does this mean, as leaders, we need to be down in the weeds micromanaging?

The answer is a simple YES. In times of great change, leaders cannot afford the luxury of delegating all of the details. The leaders need to be in the know, since it is their responsibility to "keep the crew alive". Organizations need their senior executives to know the most important things happening in the company, from cash reserves to productivity to consumer buying patterns, behavior, and desires for product or service changes.

Ken Lehman of Winning Workplaces, an organization devoted to rewarding and assisting small business excellence, had this to say about what the best businesses do when there's a financial crisis:

> Instead of cutting heads as the first response, Winning Workplaces look at maintaining critical mass but taking an across-the-board pay cut. People know you're trying to share the pain. People understand you have to be sustainable financially to

be sustainable in terms of culture and values. You have to do what you have to do, but sharing the pain is so important. I just saw something in last week's *Newsweek*: Fifty-two percent of people surveyed are cutting across the board instead of doing layoffs. The people we've honored have intuitively known to do that.

There's another harsh truth you may need to come to accept. During challenging times, the first reaction of many will be to blame leadership. You're the one holding the bag! No matter what the situation or circumstance, no matter what the external reality, you're the one who'll get the questions and the blame. Practicing letting go and focusing on what you can and cannot control can be a life-saver.

Since you have chosen the path of leadership, it's up to you to develop your ability to not take it personally. Sometimes that's easier said than done. I say that from personal experience!

Move Fluidly from Short-Term to Long-Term Thinking

Your job is to look to the short term and to set manageable, short-term goals that you can measure regularly. The results will change your next short-term goals. That said, you also need to look at the long term, because if we don't take time to look to the future, we risk becoming obsolete. The worst case with looking only at the short term during tough times is that we lose sight of long-term value creation.

To think about the long term is to be strategic, and when we are overwhelmed with the crisis of the moment it's tempting to stick with addressing what's right in front of us, rather than asking strategic questions. Strategic thinking starts with inquiry. Why are we doing what we're doing? What are the ramifications of the trajectory we are on? What scenarios should we explore?

Those leaders who don't look to the long term are not going to succeed because they are not driving the company forward into new opportunities or directions. They aren't doing one of the primary jobs of leadership, which is to look toward what will happen next, identify challenges, threats and changes that can or will impact the organization. Leaders who look to the long term are the ones who see the writing on the wall around new legislation, cultural trends, customer desires and market opportunities.

How can you actively bring a long-term perspective while you're addressing immediate issues?

1. **Link executive compensation to long-term goals, rather than short-term wins.** This is self-explanatory. We do what we are incentivized to do. We need to stop rewarding only short-term thinking, and start rewarding longer-term performance.

2. **Put your time towards the creation of a robust succession plan.** When you focus on developing the talent under you that investment of time pays off over the long term. Hiring externally is expensive, and dismisses the value of institutional knowledge brought by those talented executives who have risen up in the ranks.

3. **Ask yourself hard questions.** Remember to focus on the "why" rather than the "how".

4. **Advocate for long-term investment.** At a lecture at Nazareth College in 2009, Ron Zarella, former Chairman of Bausch and Lomb, suggested that the U.S. government impose a 75% tax on those who hold a stock for less than six months, 20% for one to three years, and 10% for more than three years. This discourages short-termism and shifts our thinking to creative, long-term solutions.

Which brings us to innovation, the lifeblood of success over the long haul…

Drive Innovation

The single most important element of Alignment when it comes to organizational impact is that it enables and forwards innovation. Using Jim Collins' language in Built to Last, to "preserve the core and stimulate progress" the CEO must focus on survival, and liberation, through innovation. In a downturn we need to continually invest in R&D, so that we can grow anew. We need to fuel a culture of innovation—a culture of Alignment.

Breakthrough innovation and breakthrough performance can happen when we reduce fear-based behavior, and when we encourage divergent thinking, reflection time, and out of-the-box ideas.

Thomas Watson, IBM's founder, said upon his retirement, "If I had it to do all over again, I would have encouraged employees to make more mistakes". Innovation thrives on dialogue, experimentation, creativity, and dreaming. If we don't let mistakes happen without punishment, if we don't encourage experimentation and dreaming, we won't get the results we want.

How do inspiring leaders drive innovation? While there are obvious things like innovation labs, R&D initiatives, and hiring external consultants to work with your existing strengths and translate them into new possibilities, there's also the simple act of asking questions that prompt great thinking.

Let's take a moment to look at some amazing innovations that started with the question: "How can we solve world problems AND deliver something people want?" They come from giant companies and small mom-and-pop start-ups alike.

Sample Innovation #1—*What is a way we could alleviate malnutrition, conquer obesity, reduce pollution, **and** deliver something delicious to global gourmets all at the same time?* Meet The Not Company, a Chilean Artificial Intelligence start-up specializing in using plants to create beautifully flavored substitutes for meat and dairy products. Chile represents the third largest market in the world for mayonnaise, so the company started there and has been creating breakthroughs by sequencing plant genomes and applying science to food creation.

Sample Innovation #2 — *What if we created something fun and energy-generating?* The Sustainable Dance Floor was created in Holland by Doll, an architectural firm, and an environmental consultancy called Enviu. They launched at a party that showcased sustainable ideas and products—and because of the huge draw for anything that could be both fun **and** sustainable, twelve hundred people showed up! The Sustainable Dance Floor is a piezoelectric floor that captures the energy of the moving dancers, and that electricity powers the lights, speakers, and other parts of the electrical system in the club. Sustainable Dance Club, the company, has created solutions that promise nightclubs a 30-percent reduction in energy consumption, 50 percent less refuse generated, and a 30 percent reduction in CO_2 emissions.[11]

Sample Innovation #3 — *What could we do to marry quality product, sustainability, and address real health concerns of customers?* LG Electronics, who for over a decade sustained leadership in market share for front loading washers and dryers in the U.S., created something that allergy sufferers everywhere would covet: the Steam Washer™ with Allergiene cycle™ and SteamDryer.™ John Herrington, former President of LG Electronics USA, Inc., Digital Appliances, says, "Our growth in front-load laundry was a direct result of listening to our consumers, and it reflected consumers' excitement about our colorful array of premium products and innovative technologies such as steam". The washer/dryer combo saves space **and** saves energy, needs no vent, **and** reduces common allergens.

Sample Innovation #4 — *What if we cut fuel usage and reduced emissions?* All of us who work in manufacturing and/or rely on shipping to get our products to or from overseas, listen up. Innovations in shipping technology are enabling cargo vessels to reduce their annual fuel usage by 10 to 35

---

[11] http://sustainablerotterdam.blogspot.com/2008/09/club-watt-worlds-first-sustainable.html 12   http://www.skysails.info/

percent. Cost savings **and** emissions savings. It's so basic— just attach a large sail to a tow rope and reduce fuel costs immediately through natural, 100 percent free wind power.[12]

It all starts with powerful questions. Just look at the many organizations that have asked "How can we contribute during a global crisis?" and shifted their factories to making masks and personal protective equipment for healthcare workers during the Covid-19 pandemic. From car interior manufacturers Zettl group (who typically supply Rolls Royce and Porche with high end leather seating) to Hanes and Los Angeles Apparel companies who are all filling a gap for healthcare workers using their existing equipment and insights from the healthcare industry. This innovation was possible because they asked the question – how can we contribute?

What are you working on that addresses world problems and gives needed purpose and meaning to your organization? Innovation doesn't happen without dreaming. If we are wound up, attempting to rush to solve problems, we're not taking the necessary time, and we're not in the necessary state, to dream.

Dreaming, activating the imagination, is a requirement for Alignment.

Conduct a Resilience Audit

All organizations have the capacity to adapt to changing circumstances, but when employees and leaders are not prepared or ready for change the best strategies can fail.

Resilience, the ability to bounce back from change or challenge, is partially hard-wired. However, resilience can also be taught and elicited through tested exercises and methods when we have the chance. What we also know from our research into Resilience at Work is that leaders tend to have higher levels of innate resilience than the people they lead. We don't know if that's because people self-select into leadership who are better at adaptation and flexibility and even relish change and challenge, or if it's that we learn to adapt better as we move up the proverbial ladder. The result of leaders having higher levels of innate change-readiness is that they can easily forget that the other people they work with will have a much harder time coping with significant change and recovering quickly.

Conducting a resilience audit for your people can be as simple as rolling out an assessment like our Resilience at Work Assessment - a self-assessment that looks at fifteen attributes of resilience, or as complex as creating focus groups and 1:1 interviews for key team members using the research on resilience and "psychological capital" and compiling the results.

Knowledge is power. Once you know the areas for development you can address those items. For example, one key attribute of resilience is optimism. If your organization is lacking optimism that can pose a massive issue when communicating about the future.

Inspire Others to Think Bigger and to Connect to Team Identity

In 1933, U.S. President Franklin Delano Roosevelt was confronted with intense challenges. At the time of his inauguration, the country was in chaos, near the very bottom of the Depression. One quarter of the population could not find work. Bread lines and desperation took over the nation.

With a unique directness, Roosevelt took a stand against fear with these immortal words:

> *This is pre-eminently the time to speak the truth, the whole truth, frankly and boldly. Nor need we shrink from honestly facing conditions in our country today. This great nation will endure as it has endured, will revive and will prosper.*

> *So, first of all, let me assert my firm belief that the only thing we have to fear is fear itself.*

The impact of that speech was galvanizing to people who were hungry, scared, and looking for leadership to get them through a difficult time.

As the leader and figurehead, your job is to use your position and visibility to inspire your employees and to raise them out of survival thinking. They need to transcend the reality of day-to-day pain and look at a bigger picture, have gratitude for the positive, and believe that better times are possible. This does not mean "shrinking from honestly facing conditions" - it means accepting what's real and focusing on the future.

Develop "Soft Power"

In the discipline of political science, there is a wonderful concept that we should move into all realms of leadership, and that concept is called "soft power". Professor Joseph Nye, former dean of the Kennedy School of Government at Harvard University, and former Assistant Secretary of Defense in the Clinton administration, coined the term 'soft power' to describe a power separate from the hard power of military and economic might, the power of a nation to attract and persuade rather than to coerce and dominate.

In business, those leaders who possess "soft" skills are the ones that attract, enroll, engage, and retain followers—who succeed in mobilizing great action in their organizations. Positive relationships to others depend on those soft skills like empathy, working well with others, willingness to give and receive help, and being appreciative of others. Command-and-control leadership is only one tool in a large toolbox. Particularly for the generations joining the workforce in this new millennium, command-and-control has gone the way of the past.

Michael Dell, CEO of Dell Computer, was confronted with some highly critical feedback in the fall of 2001. Internal interviews showed that they saw Dell as detached and impersonal, and that employees did not feel loyal to the company's leadership. The feeling in the organization was so bad that half of Dell's employees reported they would leave if they had an opportunity arise.

Bravely, Michael Dell accepted the real, and focused on the future. He set up a meeting within one week of the feedback and faced his top twenty managers, demonstrating his desire to build relationships and community. In this meeting the well-known introvert, who is not one to talk about himself, demonstrated his self-awareness by telling the group that because of his life-long shyness, he could come across as unapproachable and disengaged.

It wasn't easy, but Dell viewed this challenge as an opportunity to build new connections and buy-in. He came forward via video to every manager in the company. The result? He was able to communicate his vulnerability, and gather buy-in on a mass scale for his leadership. He is also famous for practicing discipline, and has been one of the longest-serving founder-CEOs in the history of technology companies.

When times are tough, and in my experience looking at leaders of all shapes and sizes, I find many senior executives struggle with what to express and what not to. They think that they need to have bravado: "Everything's alright. There are no problems". Leaders who are really effective are confident but also appropriately vulnerable; they are authentic. They are willing to share what's concerning them and, along with that, they're sharing their confidence that the collective group can get beyond those concerns.

Ben Palmer, entrepreneur and CEO of Genos International, Australia, found one leadership challenge more compelling than anything else in his graduate research into organizational excellence. That challenge was developing emotional intelligence in organizational leadership.

> The simple question was: to make emotional intelligence effective in the workplace, what does it need to do for you? Leaders said it needed to be simple, not too academic, and pragmatic (shifting to business language). In more academic language, we might look at neuroticism. In business, we'll talk

46

about being stable or unstable. Simple. They also wanted high face validity and credibility if we applied an emotional intelligence model. We wanted a proven approach. The research and statistics were critical for business leaders.

We've found in our research that EI can be just as important at IQ, sometimes more so. Most people in the C- suite are bright, but what distinguishes those who are beyond just smart is their emotional intelligence.

When times get tough, we need to come back to business fundamentals: reducing costs, setting goals, and managing performance. In order to get people engaged, inspire people, and manage performance, you need emotional intelligence.

An example of the importance and value of developing emotional intelligence skills, during a challenging time, occurred when a business process improvement team in India was failing. The teams was going into areas of the business and finding ways to improve efficiency and reduce costs in the way work was being completed. The people on this team were technically brilliant but emotionally unintelligent.

The problem was with the way they communicated their purpose, carried out their work, and delivered their news. As a result, instead of being seen as as people on the same team helping to get the job done better, they were seen and felt as the "business police".

The result?

A shortage of buy-in into their recommendations and suggested changes. They experienced resistance wherever they went in the business, finding it hard to get their work done because their colleagues just simply wouldn't interact with them or give them access to the information they needed.

The company decided to offer them a learning and development program based on emotional intelligence to help them build personal and interpersonal skills, and develop self-awareness, empathy, the ability to reason not only with technical but emotional information, and to manage feelings within themselves and others.

After going through the program, the business process improvement team were much better at communicating their purpose, building relationships with the areas of the business they assisted, and delivering their news in a way that facilitated positive moods and emotions.

Now they don't face the resistance they once faced, are experiencing much greater enjoyment from their work, and are getting on with making a powerful bottom-line difference in their company.

Consider this one last quote from Ben Palmer: "I find that people who really get ahead in tough times—that when the going gets tough, it's time to get both tough and soft together. As a manager, you can tell people what they have to do, or you can give them a vision and ask them what they need to get there. People get that you are their advocate".

Measure and Build Employee Engagement

The strengths revolution has resulted in a whole new wave of measurement for organizations: employee engagement. Instead of measuring attrition, stress, or problems, we can measure what we want to call attention to and build inside of our teams. That's employee engagement, which has a direct, proven correlation with productivity and retention.[12]

Tom Schultz, of Lundberg Farms, sat down with me and with the CEO emeritus of Winning Workplaces, Ken Lehman. Ken's job after many years of running a family business that pioneered people-friendly policies in the workplace, was to help determine the top small companies to work for in the United States via the Winning Workplaces awards. As the 2008 winner, Lundberg Farms has an amazing story of their leadership in the organically

---

[12] http://www.gallup.com/consulting/52/employee-engagement.aspx

grown rice category in supermarkets nationwide, and how they have measured employee engagement via retention.

Lundberg Farms was founded in 1937 by Albert and Frances Lundberg. The Sacramento Valley became the home of the former Nebraska farmers. Albert had seen the ravages of the Dustbowl that resulted from poor soil management and short-sighted farming techniques, and the family business went on to pioneer organic rice-growing in America. They believe deeply in the idea that healthy food comes from healthy soil, and that they are stewards of the land they grow on. Schultz says:

> When I first met the brothers, what struck me was how real they were; they were not enamored of their success. They didn't look for or seek any privileges. They treated people respectfully. They cared about people, particularly their community of employees. As a result we have a 90 percent or better retention rate. Our CEO does monthly meet-the-CEO forums, where he has coffee and asks what's on their mind. He then publishes the questions and challenges the management team to engage people in solving problems. We also do employee surveys on an annual basis. It helps us zero in on what's going well and where we need training and development. We do focus groups on our training and development programs, so we know how people are reacting and changing.
>
> Because of the respect we have for them, employees are incredibly loyal. Just last week an employee noticed that with twenty machines feeding rice down to the plate for a rice cake, there was a half-inch off. He figured out how to eliminate spillage—it will save at least seventy-five thousand dollars in lost rice. Employees don't think that way unless they are invested in the idea that we're in this together.
>
> Acknowledging what is and focusing on the future are the easy parts. Building community is the most important thing we do.

We believe in looking at our community very broadly. Our community is bigger than just our employees. It's our growers, our chefs, not-for-profits educating kids and feeding the hungry —we look at community from the perspective of everyone we touch through our company and our products. Looking at challenges as opportunity, in the seed of every crisis is the opportunity for growth. Sometimes in the middle of it you say you would not like so many opportunities!

When we started growing rice organically, no one was. That knowledge was lost post-WWI with the advent of agribusiness. There are two different types of weeds: aerobic and anaerobic. The anaerobic weed, called sedge, overcame the wet fields. We thought they had lost the entire crop. But we dried up the field and realized that the weeds were dead, but under the weeds they had a crop of rice. They re-flooded the field, and voila—a way to grow rice without pesticides and with less water usage.

Lundberg Farms developed a technique based on that observation—it's now in the textbooks. What a way to turn a challenge into an opportunity for innovation!

Another hurdle came when the price of conventional rice spiked. They tried to figure out what to do with their pricing. Should they go with it and maximize revenue, or should they be consistent and build over time? They gave up the opportunity to maximize short-term profit in order to build their relationship with consumers. The customers believed in this trusted brand that wouldn't gouge them, and the company grew as a result.

TRY THIS
Measure Engagement

1. Put together your own employee engagement ten-to-twenty-question survey for your direct reports. You can also use the Gallup Q12, which is a very popular and well-researched tool, or some other surveys or questions that you like.

2. Have everybody take the survey and have someone tabulate the responses.

3. Using the aggregate responses, sit down with your group and talk about the results. Discuss what is higher, what is lower. Discuss why some responses are more favorable than others.

4. Pick two items to work on. One of them should be a positive result or strength that the team wants to build. The other should be a lower score that the team wants to improve.

5. Develop a specific plan with clear accountabilities and timelines.

6. Spend time reviewing progress on that plan at least once a month with your team.

7. Take the survey again in six months or a year to measure your progress

8. Repeat the above steps until your team is perfect. Just kidding, of course!

Re-orient to the Purpose of the Organization

Every organization has a core purpose for being, even those organizations that provide widely diverse products and services. Every brand that is driven by purpose has the capacity to connect directly to a customer need. And those brands engage the people who work on them to contribute their best.

As a leader, it's your job to bring people back to why they are working there in the first place. Repeat that message as much as possible. It has the power to create Alignment.

BWX is a global natural beauty company with a portfolio of brands including Sukin, Mineral Fusion and Andalou. Founded and headquartered in Australia, BWX is on a mission worldwide. On their website you can see the clarity of their purpose: "Our goal at BWX is to make natural beauty the only choice for people wanting to live a healthy, balanced life, free from unnecessary toxins."

When the Covid-19 pandemic crisis hit, BWX consistently communicated the importance of their purpose and values.

BWX leadership confronted reality head on and viewed challenges as opportunities - ultimately speeding much needed hand-sanitizer to market at a fraction of the normal time, which was both a win for the company bottom line and for the world. They donated 1M in product to children's charities who could immediately use it as a contribution to the local community. They immediately focused on building relationships and community by getting into fast action to engage the hearts and minds of all of their employees. They set up structures to practice physical and mental discipline from creating safety protocols for factory and warehouse workers, in particular focusing on their value of wellness to create solutions for employees and their own health and wellbeing.

According to Ingrid Anderson, Chief People Officer, "Coming back to the values has been key to everything we do. First our wellness value has driven our practices with employees. We've focused on safety and hygiene from temperature checks and distancing to shifting people to remote working who can do so. We've gone above and beyond for employees still coming into work by giving them $100 grocery vouchers, providing lunches and dinners and care packages of product. We've done yoga and mindfulness sessions, created fun events even down to online fashion shows, BWX got Talent, best lockdown beard, you name it. Innovation and bravery are two of our values that have tied in well together. We have had to make difficult decisions around investment and bringing product to market so quickly, hiring people and investing in the business and in people during this time. It's amazing to see the results, including the fact that our treatment of employees builds loyalty. People are focused and in attendance. Absenteeism is low. Not one person has taken advantage of our pandemic leave policy. Putting our values front and center helps our people live by those values of wellness, innovation, diversity, bravery and respect."

Preserve Your Own Optimism and Energy for the Task at Hand

As the leader, your first job is to preserve yourself. Without your own energy and fortitude, it's hard to lead your organization where you want it to go. Remember the oxygen mask on an airplane analogy - you can't help someone else until your own mask is on.

A few years back, I was a participant in a Cambridge University retreat called the Prince of Wales Business and the Environment Programme. As a leader in my own organization and someone who works with leaders, I felt that it was important for me to truly understand issues of sustainability in business, and how our economies are being impacted by climate change.

After four days with experts from around the world, I felt overwhelmed, depressed, and fearful about the future, and I was no fun to be around. I felt overwhelmed by the massive nature of what we are collectively facing, and incapable of doing much about it as an individual. It was a dark night of the soul. If I was going to inspire anyone, it wasn't going to be from a place of disempowerment or despair.

How can we energize people to focus on the emergencies we are facing? How can we get people out of their own self-interest in order to get their best contributions to the bigger picture of saving ourselves from disaster? How will we get the political will, the will of corporate leadership, to focus on aligning the goals of our organizations with the needs of humanity?

I had to make a commitment to action for my organization. Rather than being depressed, I had to get my own energy back and figure out some next steps that would educate and engage my team in how we might address these issues inside of our organization and then how we might help other leaders to do the same. It's been a challenge, but our organization has committed to carbon neutrality, a fully paperless operation, annual tree planting as well as annual triple bottom line measurement. Since we began that trajectory, hundreds of thousands of others have as well, and that makes a true impact.

TRY THIS
Preserving Your Optimism

This exercise is from Martin Seligman's wonderful work on "Learned Optimism". Because it is such a fabulous and simple exercise, I give it to nearly every executive I work with to use on themselves and with their teams.

In order to help others believe in the possibility or probability of a positive future, you need to believe it yourself. How can you build your optimism, even in the face of great adversity?

Building optimism on a regular basis makes you happier and more content with your life—and makes you a more effective and resilient leader. Research suggests that this exercise's positive effects continue six months after starting it. In order to maintain the positive effects, the exercise needs to be repeated at least weekly.

Instructions

At the end of each day, write down three things that went well that day. These things can be small in importance ("My computer booted up right away this morning when I turned it on") or large ("I was offered the job I had interviewed for today"). After each positive event, answer this question, "Why did this good thing happen?" When we visit and revisit the "why," we begin to see our impact on positive outcomes and to repeat positive behaviors.

Example

Good Thing	Why Did It Happen?
I solved a complex dilemma for a client.	I've been working hard and focusing.
My shoulder is feeling better.	I've been following my doctor's recommendations.

Take a moment and think of three good things that happened today. Attribute that positive to something and see how it changes your perception of your own power to make positive things happen. Repeat daily!

Good Thing	Why Did It Happen?
1	
2	
3	

The good news for leaders is that it is absolutely possible to lead productive, highly engaged teams through challenge and crisis…but what about managing your own response to circumstances beyond your control? How can you best lead yourself out of fear or reactivity?

Chapter 4

Alignment: Your Personal How-To Guide

"Nothing in life is to be feared. It is only to be understood."

—Marie Curie

Whether you are in senior leadership, or an individual contributor, and you feel yourself operating from fear, what does it take to step into an empowered way of living and working?

It takes looking at our own fear, and it takes practice at Alignment.

Our culture of constant stimulation, twenty-four-hour connectivity, volatile markets, job losses, and general stress makes it all the more important to consciously choose a different way of operating. We forget how incredibly powerful we are.

What would happen if you got out of fear and took a chance on life, as an individual, as a leader, or as a whole organization? There are limitless possibilities out there! Re-examine your options. Dream big. Be optimistic about something that might seem risky—and know that it will result in getting you somewhere good. You do have a choice until you don't.

You have the freedom to focus your attention wherever you choose. Sometimes we don't consciously take charge of our amazing ability to choose where we put our time, energy, and engagement. What we focus on has an impact on how we think and how we see the world. If you choose to focus only on what's wrong, the world looks like a pretty ugly place. If you choose to consciously focus on what's right, what's working, what you can expand, build upon, replicate, or grow—that has its own power.

Barbara Frederickson is a distinguished professor and researcher, as well of the author of a popular book, *Positivity*. As a social psychologist, Frederickson conducts research in positive psychology and positive emotions. She coined the "broaden and build" theory of positive emotions. She found that people who experience positive emotions show heightened levels of creativity, inventiveness, and big-picture perceptual focus, and that positive emotions play a role in long-term psychological resilience and flourishing.[13] So here's the rub.

The tipping-point ratio for positivity is three to one. We need three positive emotions to every one negative to flourish in life, and to be open to possibility. Fear closes us down and positivity opens us up.

In a business setting, we are often well trained to use our critical eye. It is the view of reality that looks for what's not working, what needs to be fixed, for problems to be solved. And it's useful and valuable, but not without a counterbalance, the appreciative eye.

That is the view that looks for what IS working, what is positive, what is possible. If we can maintain a three-to-one ratio at work, favoring the appreciative eye to the critical eye, we maintain a healthy, innovative, and productive working environment.

Looking at the four practices of Alignment allows us to tackle fear from all angles, and to broaden and build positivity. We can remind the body how to relax and function at its peak, we can help the mind construct new, more positive beliefs, and we can allow our emotions to be expressed in a healthy way, informing but not dictating our actions. Again, the four practices are:

- Accepting what is, and focusing on the future

- Building relationships and community

- Viewing challenges as opportunities

- Practicing physical and mental discipline

---

[13] Fredrickson, B. L., "The Value of Positive Emotions," *American Scientist*, 91, 330-335, 2003

Accepting What Is and Focusing on the Future

It's a tough sell to tell businesspeople that they need to accept things the way they are. We're high achievers, 'Type A's, and we never back down from a challenge or believe that something's not possible, right?

One of the great paradoxes of leadership is the fact that we need to push forward and believe that things are possible, AND we have to accept reality when it hits us in the face. We already know bad things happen, but sometimes we just don't want to believe it.

An acquaintance of mine is a very talented creative and incredible artist within the fashion industry. For many years, she poured heart and soul into a high-end clothing boutique that was very dear to her, but it was not successful in making a profit. When the 2008 recession began, her clientele dwindled and she could no longer break even. After sacrificing her home to pay business debts, she had come to the end of a long road. She had to accept the reality that despite her love of her work, this specific venture had not succeeded, and she needed to do something new.

If we don't accept what is, we can't move forward.

Is there is a reality you are having trouble accepting, or that your organization is having trouble accepting?

TRY THIS
Accepting Reality

Think for a moment of the landscape of your work. What realities do you need to accept as fact? What are you not being honest about with yourself or your colleagues? Is there something that is not working that needs to:

a. be changed

b. be destroyed to free up energy for something new?

c. is there someone you need to say something to that you haven't?

d. is there a reality that you have been ignoring because you haven't had the time to focus on it?

Examples of what you may want to accept so that you or your organization can move forward:

- Your core products and services are not relevant during a pandemic.

- The division you work in is in crisis and hasn't been adding value to the business. Morale is low.

- Your right-hand person is not performing after a death in her family.

- The price of manufacturing has risen based on rising resource prices, and the model for retail pricing is now off.

- Company branding that works well in the U.S. is offensive to people in Asia, and no one noticed before the product launch.

- Everyone on your team is tired because they've been overworking.

We are all part of an ever-changing planet that grows, changes, dies, and is born in other forms. We are always changing, no matter how much we think we stay the same. Think of yourself when you were seven years old. How similar or different are you to that seven-year-old child? You are not just different in your thinking and your actions, but you're entirely different on a cellular level.

There is a famous Buddhist teaching—think of every person you know or have ever known, and imagine that one hundred years from now, none of them will be alive, and there will be a whole new group of people on the earth where they used to be. That teaching helps us to remember that change is a constant—that everything is impermanent, an ever-moving stream. To accept impermanence helps us to reduce our suffering and recognize the truth of the human condition.

Tibetan Buddhist monks have a special tradition of making intricate, ornate paintings out of sand or butter, and once they are complete, they are destroyed with the wave of an arm or by melting in the sun. They are a representation of impermanence; everything has a lifecycle, including us. When we start to normalize change, instead of pushing against it, we can go with it. We can accept the reality that no matter how much we like something the way it is, it will evolve, become different in some way.

When we start to normalize change, we can also start to play, envision, and create. We can begin to choose what kind of future we want to base our actions on. Inventors of all kinds are just people who cultivate this natural ability to dream of a different future.

Close your eyes for a moment and imagine yourself five minutes from now. That's one easy way to get you into a future-visioning state. Take another moment and think of something you would like to happen. There are plenty of ways to dream of a positive future. This exercise requires you to step into the future as if it has already happened.

Building Relationships and Community

"Imagine a community where we all want the absolute best for each other. And actually, we can also expect that every other single person wants the best for us."

—*Robert Thurman*

Let's think for a moment about the consequences of isolation.

In a world where we're becoming increasingly connected online, we're becoming increasingly disconnected from a deeply felt sense of belonging.

As affluence grows in western democracies, people become more self-involved and disconnected from their communities. They choose to have conversations with people just like them, or to create limited relationships that don't challenge thinking or cultivate curiosity or debate. We may begin to demonize people who don't think like we do, and to dampen our civil discourse and desire to understand diverse perspectives. Pathologies arise from this disconnection like narcissism and dissociation. Ultimately our worldview becomes polarized, and empathy and compassion are thrown out and replaced by a disdain for who we perceive as the "other". Vitriolic criticism of others has become commonplace even in news broadcasts that used to be a neutral source of factual information. **We need to break out of these damaging patterns, because our lack of connection is impacting our desire to give of ourselves for the betterment of others.**

The week I started to write this book, I went on a road trip across the American Southwest with two old friends, Mike and Andy. I started seeing the opportunity for Alignment everywhere—and, in particular, through the lens of dealing with the transformations and changes in our individual lives.

Mike and I have known each other since I was eighteen and he was twenty. At the time we met, he was my boss twice over—as the manager of the radio station I volunteered at as a disc jockey, and at the local record store, The Mad Platter. That's when there were still records but I digress!

The impetus of the trip was the early passing of Mike's wife Weibke. Mike and Weibke, both history professors, had been living in Maine and he needed to get to Los Angeles. Through the miracle of Facebook, he had connected to old friends, and would be visiting many of them along the way. We would start in Texas and end our drive together in Las Vegas, a place that is not number one on my vacation list, but was somehow appropriate—a place as unsustainable as possible, a mirage in the desert.

Weibke was someone who represented Alignment to me—she adapted easily to different cultures but retained her individuality and spirit. I have a distinct memory of their wedding on the cliffs above the Pacific Ocean in San Francisco. Weibke wore white, with sneakers and a jean jacket. A story Mike told me about how Weibke dealt with her cancer always amazed me; after she would go to chemo, she'd sometimes go on a long walk or jog.

Andy was also in a place of change—he had just returned from four months in India, completing a long cycle of yoga teacher training, and he had met someone new. In six weeks they were engaged and he was taking the big plunge: moving, starting his own yoga studio, and getting married.

As for me, I was also on the verge of starting a new life, with an adoption in the works. If it all went well, the next year would bring my husband and I a new daughter and we would be first-time parents of a young toddler.

At this crossroads between phases of our lives, Andy, Mike, and I drove toward the future with a combination of grief, joy of being together, and fear of the unknown. It was great to be with each other. We human beings are gifted with the ability to deal with incredible pain along with incredible joy—sometimes all mixed together. Part of developing Alignment is remembering we are not alone, that we are all connected in this human experience, that we all have times of suffering and times of joy, and we are truly in the same boat. When we have connections to other people, our ability to operate from our strength, increases.

Plain and simple, we need each other. Without community, we are nothing. There is an African philosophy called Ubuntu. Ubuntu reminds us that we are interconnected and interdependent. Bishop Desmond Tutu describes it with the words: "We think of ourselves far too frequently as just individuals, separated from one another, whereas you are connected and what you do affects the whole world. When you do well, it spreads out; it is for the whole of humanity". One of the great lessons of Ubuntu is that leaders owe their status to the will of the people under them. This attitude is what has made so many leaders successful during crises and deep change.

When we look on our relationship to others, it's our ability to build relationship and community that will serve us during challenging times. Great leaders know that they need to build relationships and a shared sense of purpose. Think right now of a leader you admire. Chances are they are excellent at building relationships and surrounding themselves with smart people they can trust.

To experience Alignment, we need to remember that we need other people. We need to build relationships and community.

TRY THIS
Identify Your Support Team

One simple way to build relationships and community is to identify people who matter to you, both personally and professionally. Who is your support team? Who do you spend your time with? Who do you need to help you be successful? And two last questions: What's missing for you in this arena, and whom can you reach out to?

FAMILY AND FRIENDS	Family and friends might include people from your extended community; church, volunteer organizations, school friends, parents' associations, or political groups.
WORK	Your work team might include your boss, colleagues, direct reports, customers, vendors, consultants
ADVOCATES	Many of us forget this critical category of advocates. Who is there specifically to help you? A coach, mentor, spiritual leader, counsellor, teacher, or guide.

As you look at your Support Team, how many of the people who matter to you are at work? How are you building relationships and community in that part of your life? When we focus all our interpersonal energies at home, we lose out on one of the most powerful, most exciting opportunities we have for high-functioning workplaces.

We know that when we have close relationships at work, it is more fun, less frustrating, and just plain nicer to come to work every day. When we have a place we can vent, a place to dream, a place to share, it changes the quality of our work output as well.

Working and living at a distance—in our immediately virtual world of global shutdowns and self-isolation—can make building relationships and community more difficult. So, first things first! When you're operating at a distance—do watch your social media intake. Anecdotal evidence shows that too much time spent on social media platforms can reinforce isolation and make us feel lonely, anxious and depressed. Anonymous comments from strangers can be vicious and degrading, and taking in too much criticism is truly damaging to us. Disconnection can make us self-focused and create within us a lack of desire to contribute to the well-being of others.

Viewing Challenges as Opportunities

The cornerstone of positive psychology is the ability for us to take what comes to us and find the good within it.

A client I'll call Larry founded a specialty research firm. That company grew quickly, and within four years was acquired by a large firm with an established brand and reputation. After a year, Larry was beset by doubts and strain. He didn't feel built to deal with the pressures of a large corporation. His decisions were consistently vetoed by the CEO of the parent company, and Larry felt he had lost all his power. He was unhappy with the direction the organization was taking.

He concluded it was time for direct action. He met with his executive team, and decided to make a proposal to buy back the organization. After months of planning, and a presentation he felt was excellent, the parent organization rejected his proposal. At first, he was devastated.

Larry needed to turn this challenge into an opportunity, and he did just that. The team accepted the reality that they would be part of the larger company, and set out to do award winning work and use the infrastructure of the big organization to publicize their achievements. They became a force of nature, winning a series of industry awards. Larry was able to adapt to the new environment and take on something he'd never imagined.

Think of an experience that at the time was very difficult, but later you were able to learn from.

TRY THIS

Reframing Journaling Exercise

What negative experiences are you on the other side of?

How did they help you grow?

What have they added to your life?

Take ten minutes to explore on paper.

What did you learn from your challenging experience?

Practicing Physical and Mental Discipline

Physical and mental discipline comprise the most basic level of self-care. If we don't have that covered, we can't keep ourselves in a positive, healthy state of mind and body.

Remember that we humans are hard-wired to respond to threats in three ways: fight, flight, or freeze.[14] The physical signs of fear include racing heartbeat, dry mouth, wide eyes with pupils dilated, and energized muscles. There is a physiological chain reaction in the fight-or-flight response.

The brain takes in the stimulus and the amygdala (a small, almond-shaped structure in your mid-brain) makes a decision—is this something to be afraid of? The autonomic nervous system has two branches—the sympathetic, which helps us deal with stress by initiating our fight, flight, freeze response, and the parasympathetic, which relaxes us. When the sympathetic nervous system fires off, the adrenal glands release adrenaline and other hormones, the heart speeds up, your blood pressure rises, your lungs breathe faster to circulate more oxygen, your digestive system and immune system slow down, and your muscles get ready to go.

We may begin with a freeze response, in which we stop whatever we were occupied with and become hyper-vigilant or hyper-alert. The next response in sequence might be to attempt to flee. Fleeing can mean running away literally or by dissociating or feeling separate from the physical body. Fighting means using our aggression to attempt control of the situation, be it physical fighting, verbal attack, or even a menacing look.

If this is what happens to us when we experience fear, what does it mean that we spend so much time in this state? What happens to the body? We might get headaches, we may have problems sleeping or relaxing, and we may feel anxiety, tension, anger, depression, or lack of focus or concentration. We might have sexual dysfunction, suppressed immunity, and skin ailments. We may shun food, have an increase in appetite, or lose our interest in normal activities.

Chronic stress can be harmful to your brain. Sonia J. Lupien, Ph.D., a research scientist at the Centre for Studies on Human Stress, University of

---

14 Cannon, WB: *Bodily Changes in Pain, Hunger, Fear and Rage: An Account of Recent Research Into the*
Function of Emotional Excitement, 2nd ed. New York, Appleton-Century-Crofts, 1929

Montreal, says, "Many studies show the negative impact of stress on physical health, such as blood pressure, heart disease, etc., but few address the effects on mental health. Our studies look directly at the long-term effects of stress, or stress hormones, on brain function".

Dr. Lupien's research found that individuals with high levels of the stress hormone cortisol performed poorly on memory tests and had a measurably smaller hippocampus (part of the brain responsible for memory and learning). When we stay too much in a state of anxiety, stress, or fear, we do damage to our physical health and well-being. We also train ourselves to remain hyper-vigilant, and it becomes a vicious circle.

If multiple people in our organizations are suffering from future shock, fear, and chronic stress, it means we are losing our ability to focus, think, and create positive outcomes. Imagine a whole company in fight, flight, or freeze, and you'll see what I see every day as a consultant—organizations with incredible capacity for serving the world that are stopped in their tracks, surviving for the short term rather than thriving over the long haul.

The good news is that we are just as hard-wired to relax, calm down, and to experience life from Alignment as we are to respond to threats with the fight, flight or freeze response, but it requires physical and mental discipline. When we care for ourselves first, we have the energy and health to tackle what comes our way. Physically, exercise and self-care go a long way toward reducing fear-based reactions.

How fast we forget when we are involved in work that we need a break every ninety minutes or so to stay at optimum productivity. We also need to keep ourselves healthy, or nothing else matters, because we're back down Maslow's hierarchy to survival, and that gets our fear into overdrive.

TRY THIS
Take a Walk or Run Outside

No matter what your fitness level, a good jaunt outside is a great option to discharge any excess energy, to get your heart going, and to get out of fight, flight, or freeze mode.

Walking thirty minutes a day can help you maintain your weight, build strong bones, keep your cardiovascular system healthy and your lymph system pumping.

Walking around the block can give you a great mental and physical re-set, and can offer you some think time as well.

Notice the world around you. Walking can also jar us out of our narrow focus, and expand our worldview.

Don't wimp out because of bad weather—take your winter coat, your umbrella, or your sun hat along.

Practicing mental discipline might mean keeping a daily list of what needs doing, which you look at and edit each morning. That kind of regular attention to your work and life pays dividends beyond getting things done; it helps us to remain calm, focused, and relaxed.

More than keeping a daily journal, practicing discipline might also mean going to exercise class or reading the newspaper with a cup of coffee. These may not look as heavy duty as training for a marathon might be, but we all have our own levels of self-care, and they should all be respected. You know what feeds your body and soul, what lets you feel nourished on a daily basis. Small bits of structure like eating at the same time every day and practicing the small, regular actions mentioned above can help you feel your own stability in the face of change.

TRY THIS

Brainstorm Which Discipline is Right for You

Do you need more physical exercise? More mental discipline to keep you positive? Are you disciplined about your physical health but terrible with letting your work suffer? Discipline makes things happen and gives us structure to fall back on. Do you have specific structures that need to be in place that aren't?

Take a moment to think about the kind of discipline that will keep you focused, healthy, and productive. The items below are a broad range and include both personal and professional considerations. They're all important—whatever makes your work better is the right discipline for you.

Examples:

exercise	keeping a to-do list	taking time for myself after work
cleaning off my desk at the end of each day	managing my calendar	reading business journals so I'm informed
monitoring my caffeine	celebrating wins	keeping notes on my employees to inform their performance to inform their performance reviews
measuring results	eating healthy	

I am one of those people who have a hard time just relaxing. The first time I tried to meditate I was in my early twenties. A work friend of mine from Taiwan invited me to her storefront temple in the Bay Area for a fire ceremony. It included many hours of meditation and there were monks chanting and lots of "smells and bells"—incense and clanging gongs—before the intensive meditation started. My first sit was a combo platter of my legs falling asleep and my attempts to massage out the pins and needles every thirty minutes or so, and my mind racing with obsessive thoughts—most of which were 'When will this end?'. We left very early—about three hours into the event—but I felt like I'd been there for a week.

So, it was all the more miraculous that after this experience, I tried again.

As a part of my stay at a health clinic in Iowa to deal with fatigue and stress, I had signed up for a four-day process of learning transcendental meditation. I had been told by the doctors that the meditation would certainly be a big part of addressing my health issues and that it would be an excellent way to spend my time forty minutes a day while I was on retreat. I had no idea if this would work for me, but what the heck? I decided to try. What else was I going to do in the middle of the Iowa cornfields? I took long walks over the quiet Iowa landscape, read books, and committed to learning to really meditate.

I closed my eyes, started my mantra and a whole new world opened up to me! I couldn't believe how easy it was. I was calm. Every so often a thought would float in, and then the mantra would float back and push it out. My breath slowed and I could feel my body completely relax. I didn't feel time pass, but I would open my eyes after exactly twenty minutes just as I'd intended, with no alarm or cue. Twenty minutes was nothing— what was I thinking before that I couldn't do twenty minutes?

After a week of meditating for twenty minutes twice a day, I started to feel different. Colors looked sharper. I was noticing sounds I hadn't heard before. My thinking was getting clearer. I was paying attention. I was mindful. Other benefits meditation can provide include improved cardiovascular health, improved brain function, and reduction of anxiety, high blood pressure, risks of diabetes, obesity, hypertension and stroke.

The American Psychological Association shows significant positive long-term benefits.[15] I have met many meditators who look at least ten years

---

[15] http://www.tm.org/research

younger than their biological age, and they credit the deep rest of meditation with their youth and longevity.

TRY THIS
Meditation Experiment

As a former "not enough time and can't sit still" person, my challenge to you is to learn one meditation technique, try it for a week, and see if it doesn't give you more time, help you to sit still and concentrate, and add enormously to your health, well-being, and sense of productivity. It may also stop you from taking the stress of work, home to your family—an added bonus! Popular Meditation Techniques:

- Prayer: Prayer can be very powerful, from recitation of a prayer or hymn that you know well, to free form silent connection to God or deity. Most major religions include prayer in some form.

- Free writing for fifteen minutes: Taking time to express ourselves quietly in writing can offer insight, relaxation, a place to vent, and a place to comfort ourselves.

- Being in nature: Taking the time to dive into our natural environment has multiple rewards. When we take time to be in nature, we give our minds time to contemplate and observe.

- Vipassana meditation: Vipassana, which means "to see things as they are" aims at eradicating mental impurities. It is a technique of observation of the self, including our thoughts and our physical sensations.

- Transcendental meditation: Popularized in the west by rock stars like the Beatles, transcendental meditation is from the Vedic tradition. It is practiced by closing the eyes and internally reciting a mantra.

- Guided visualization: Recorded visualizations can enhance creativity, focus our mind, and calm the body. It's often used by professional athletes and entertainers to envision positive performance.

- Primordial sound meditation: Deepak Chopra, once a part of the transcendental meditation tradition, has popularized his own version of an ancient mantra-based meditation.

- Brain entrainment: Binaural beats are sounds that create a brain phenomenon called brain entrainment. They are used in some hypnotic recordings, and result in a relaxation response.

- Hypnosis: Hypnosis can be used to break bad habits, uncover barriers to achievement, or to calm the mind.

Meditation doesn't just calm the nervous system; it activates the brain. Your body shifts into a deeply restful state, deeper than deep sleep, yet you are awake. Your blood pressure decreases, your muscles relax, and your breath slows along with your heart rate. In three minutes, oxygen consumption drops steeply.16

A former executive coaching client of mine who is in a very senior position at a high stress company had this to say about his newly developed meditation habit:

> At work I have to meditate at least once a day or I'm just not productive. I start reacting and not thinking. If I take that fifteen minutes, close the door, and tell my assistant I am not to be disturbed, it makes all the difference. I have started telling my team what I'm doing and now when they see me stressed out, they encourage me to take a break and do my meditation because they can see the difference!

Mental Discipline, Beliefs, Attitudes and Actions

Our beliefs shape our reality. Take a moment to think about the core beliefs that you operate on.

Negative core beliefs are deeply held views about yourself, others, or the world as a whole. They are broad and shape our thinking and our responses to life and work. Identifying them can be easier said than done because often our core beliefs are unconscious.

---

16 http://www.lorinroche.com/page4/page106/page106.html

TRY THIS

Fill in the Blanks to Explore Core Beliefs

This exercise is adapted from the wonderful Alfred Adler, who is the father of modern social psychology. Looking at how we fill in the blanks can help us understand our basic stance toward ourselves, others, our work, and the world in general. When we understand our core beliefs, we can look for evidence that either supports or does not support them. We have a choice.

I am _____.

Other people are _____.

My work is _____.

The world is _____.

I am responsible for _____.

Example of a negative stance:

> I am <u>dissatisfied</u>.
>
> Other people are <u>challenging for me to deal with</u>.
>
> My work is <u>stressful</u>.
>
> The world is <u>a difficult place we must learn to survive in</u>.
>
> I am responsible <u>for myself.</u>

Example of a more neutral to positive stance:

> I am <u>a son, a father, a husband, and a leader.</u>
>
> Other people are <u>a mixed bag</u>.
>
> My work is <u>engaging</u>.
>
> The world is <u>full of places I want to go.</u>
>
> I am responsible for <u>my family's well being</u>.

EXAMPLES	I AM	OTHERS ARE	THE WORLD IS
POSITIVE CORE BELIEFS	Grateful.	Helpful.	A complex and beautiful place to explore.
NEGATIVE CORE BELIEFS	Sad and lonely.	Uncaring.	Coming to an end any time now.
MIXED CORE BELIEFS	Growing and changing.	A mixed bag. Some good/ some bad.	Challenging but there is a lot of possibility.

If you find that any of your answers are negative, these core beliefs can be changed by challenging them effectively and building ones that are more positive. To challenge a core belief, start collecting evidence that refutes it. For example, if you believe that your work is unsatisfying and miserable, take a week to gather evidence to the contrary. Find moments of joy or engagement and notice them. Search for satisfaction.

Behaviors and attitudes rooted in fear may lean toward pessimism, obsessive thinking, mental confusion, or denial. How do we get ourselves out of each of these? Get conscious. Notice your thinking, your behavior, and how your core beliefs are shaping your actions.

Our twenty-four/seven news cycle goes to great lengths to get our attention, and by doing so, unconsciously drives up our anxiety. An already traumatic event can be pumped up with graphics, music, titles, and constant repetition. I was in the airport once and the TV monitor started blaring: CRISIS IN THE AIR! Everyone's hair stood on end before we saw that it was just about a celebrity being booted off of an airplane for intoxication. Well, that headline certainly got us to look.

Don't get me wrong—getting information is positive. Being informed is one half of the game. After we have our information, though, we need to ask questions and get into action around that information. What do we believe? What do we choose to focus our attention on?

When we are constantly in the mode of receiving information, we forget how powerful we are to create and act. My challenge to you is:

Only focus on news items upon which you are willing to take action.

Passive receiving of information kills our power. Active receiving of information builds it back.

TRY THIS
Acting on Media Input

Version One: One day per week, remove yourself from all forms of media that engage your pessimism, obsessive thinking, fear, or doubt. This may mean no social media/ internet news, television, or news radio. Take the day off from input.

During this day, instead of taking in something, create something yourself. Write your own article. Make your own movie. Take time for much-needed reflection. Take a walk. Talk to a friend. How does this input shape your thinking? What messages are you taking in on a daily basis? Where do you need to place your attention in order to think clearly and calmly?

Version Two: One day per week, with every news story you take in, make a conscious decision which actions you will take based on any new information you're getting. An action can be as simple as taking time to think about something and how it will impact your life or your organization.

Reducing obsessive thinking, when you feel your mind spinning and not stopping, is a huge challenge in our culture of "get it done right now!" I know that when I'm off my game, I can spend just as much time worrying about getting something done as I spend doing it.

One technique to stop obsessive thinking is to practice mindfulness. In simple terms, mindfulness consists of paying attention to an experience from moment to moment—without drifting into thoughts of the past, concerns about the future, or getting caught up in thoughts or opinions about what's going on. It is non-judgmental or pre-judgmental interaction with our internal and external environment. It is based upon repeated practice and real-life experience that you can activate at any time.

TRY THIS
Easy Mindfulness Practices

Throughout the day and before you go to sleep, take in a series of breaths. Instead of allowing your mind to wander over the day's concerns, direct your attention to your breathing; focus on the breath, concentrating on the feeling in the body, on the repetitive motion. Be mindful of the breath.

Pay attention to your breathing or your environment when the phone rings, when you get an email, or when there is a knock on the door. I have my computer configured to announce the time on the hour, and at that time, I remember to be mindful.

Eat a meal in a quiet place with no distractions. Focus on the look, texture, taste, and smell of the food. Notice if it feels good going down. Notice the environment and how it impacts your digestion and interest in your food.

Find a task that you do impatiently or unconsciously (i.e., waiting at a crosswalk or red light, standing in line, or washing the dishes) and concentrate on the experience as it is happening. Pay attention to sensory details: sight, sound, smell, touch, and taste. Fully experience the sensation of slowing down for that moment.

Confusion or denial can be by-products of the flight-or-freeze responses to fear. Confusion can come from not being able to distinguish our emotional response from our logical response to what's happening around us, or from the kind of mental cloudiness that stops us from moving forward and works to freeze our thinking and our actions.

TRY THIS
Clearing Up Confusion

Clearing up confusion can be as simple as taking the time needed for reflecting on whatever challenges are in front of you. Try this simple exercise, or design your own reflection time that lets you explore, for at least ten minutes.

Take a sheet of paper or journal. Don't try this on the computer, which restricts your ability to doodle, draw, or to express yourself physically in your writing. This exercise is derived from the concept of "Morning Pages," popularized by author Julia Cameron.

For ten to fifteen minutes, keep your pen or pencil moving on the page. Write anything that comes to mind. You can construct a series of questions that you need to answer, or you can just write to dump out anything that is in the way of your clear thinking.

If you have more time, stop after your first fifteen minutes then take a short break and go back to the paper for another ten minutes. You'll be surprised at how much mental confusion goes away after this short, focused time.

Denial protects us from knowing what it is painful to know. It helps us get through challenges and to stay focused and calm. But denial doesn't stay useful for long. At some point we need to stop ignoring and start paying attention—accepting the real and focusing on the future.

TRY THIS
Getting Out of Denial

Getting out of denial, shut-down, or illusion can be painful. In this case, no pain, no gain! Ask yourself the following questions:

- How am I deceiving myself?

- What have I not yet acknowledged that I need to?

- What fantasy am I keeping alive that I need to let go of?

- What reality am I being forced to accept at this time?

Semira had to accept the real. As an insurance executive managing a large team, she was faced with budget cuts and layoffs and a rapidly decreasing sense of employee morale. When I asked her to answer these questions here's what she said:

> How am I deceiving myself? I am keeping myself from acknowledging the reality that I am going to have to choose who needs to go, and that I am going to have to tell people I've worked with for 10 plus years that their roles will be eliminated.

> What have I not acknowledged that I need to? That Jeannie, one of my closest friends in the organization, will need to find another role in the company or she's out. I am keeping the fantasy alive that something will change immediately and I'll have a new budget for the next fiscal year, and that I can avoid dealing with this for the time being.

> I have to accept the reality that I can't change the way people are buying insurance from our organization, and that we need people with a new and different skill set.

When Semira took the time to really confront the reality, it started her thinking about how she could help her colleagues look elsewhere in the organization to use their skills. For some, it was not an option, but for others the advance notice Semira opted to give them was a gift.

Practicing Discipline and the Emotions

Raw, uncomfortable, out of control: when we feel this way, it's time to take an inventory. Emotionally, in order to let go of fear, we have to purge ourselves of whatever emotions of shame, sadness, anger, or loss are resident in us. Part of what we know is that emotions have both physical and mental components. Thoughts beget feelings. Our physical state shapes our emotional state. When we practice physical and mental discipline, we have a profound impact on our emotions.

In order to practice Alignment, we need to be aware of our emotional selves, and to fall on the side of happiness, joy, and good feeling. Those feelings empower us, motivate us, and help us to thrive in all that we do. There are techniques that can help us stay disciplined around our emotions, that can help us purge negative and difficult emotional states, and to cultivate positive emotions. How do we clean house emotionally?

Let's look at two uncomfortable emotional triggers that we can face that relate to shame: embarrassment and defeat. The goal is to take the charge out of the memory or situation you are facing, and the way to do so is to stop avoiding and start letting it out. Emotions, like shame, attack our basic belief about our own goodness. In order to keep ourselves out of being unconsciously ruled by our emotions, we need to process them and remember this is just another component of physical and mental discipline. Embarrassment and defeat are two uncomfortable emotional states that we can learn from and clear ourselves of.

Embarrassment

It could be that you were publicly called out at work for something you did or didn't do, or you were caught in something you didn't want anyone to know about or see.

Defeat

We all experience it at some point. We have failed, lost, or been taken down. Our thoughts drag us down and trap us in a feeling of hopelessness and disempowerment. We may be reeling from a loss and can't let go of the feeling that there is something deeply wrong with us, with someone else, with the big world. When we have no hope, it is time to face how we deal with defeat.

TRY THIS
Honoring Defeat or Embarrassment

This is equally effective as a writing exercise, or as a dialogue with someone else who has felt the impact of a defeat or embarrassment personally or professionally. This is your invitation to let it out, and let it go.

- How have you been defeated?

- How can you honor that defeat in a way that serves you?

- Is there something you feel ashamed of that you need to let go?

- What have you learned?

- How have you had to grow or change as a result?

- What is your commitment to yourself or others going forward?

Another set of emotions that we can learn to process is comprised of sadness and loss. Sadness and loss are there for a reason, just like every other emotion. The information provided by sadness or loss is a sharp focus on what is meaningful or valuable to us. We may need to experience grief and sadness over a long period of time. It's not about a quick fix; it's about honoring our emotions, learning from them, and practicing the discipline we need in order to stay healthy and to cultivate Alignment.

Like all other emotions, anger can be useful. When we want something to change, anger is our warning signal: This has to change now! Again, if it dictates our behavior, anger is damaging. If it provides information, and powers our conscious decisions to act, then it's of the greatest value. To get rid of anger or irritation, you may want to bring in that physical level again and start your endorphins flowing with a good workout.

Physical, mental, and emotional drains keep us from our greatest strengths. Take a moment and think about the last time you felt truly free, joyful, unencumbered, and creative. Invite that feeling into your leadership and into your team. Take time for frivolity! Laugh too loud! Sing in the shower! Do the touchdown dance even when you lose! Begin something you've always wanted to start. Forget the cynicism of the moment and imagine the innocent joy of childhood, when there were endless opportunities to imagine and play (or take time to watch some children, who even in the most horrific circumstances can jump into their imagination and play with joy and abandon).

TRY THIS
Getting the Feelings Out—A Healthy Vent

Constantly venting might be a very unhealthy activity because it fuels the fire of your negative feelings and negative thoughts, promoting behavior that is reactive. That said, there is such a thing as a very healthy vent! This can be done with a friend, or on paper. If you are with a friend, the key is that they are not allowed to give input; they are only allowed to say, "What else?" until you are all finished (anything that engages with a vent is colluding with your negative thoughts and feelings).

Step One — Set aside at least fifteen minutes for your vent.

Step Two — Start talking or writing. Get all of your emotions out. Talk about why you feel how you feel, talk about all the elements of it, talk about the layers of feeling, anything in there that is bothering you, making you feel angry, sad, upset, irritated, depressed, or fearful. When you start to get quiet, your friend can ask, "What else?" or you can ask yourself and write some more.

Step Three — Stop when it is all out. Take a moment to check in with how you feel then. If the answer is "calm," "relieved," "de-stressed," or "better," your work is done.

These exercises can help us through any change, but then there is crisis, the kind of change that shakes us to our core and makes us doubt our own power to prevail. How do we activate our Alignment in crisis circumstances?

Chapter 5
Crisis, Challenge, and Alignment

"The leaders I met, whatever walk of life they were from, whatever institutions they were presiding over, always referred back to the same failure, something that happened to them that was personally difficult, even traumatic, something that made them feel that desperate sense of hitting bottom—as something they thought was almost a necessity."

—*Warren G. Bennis*

Like a lot of people from New York say, it was a beautiful morning. I had a speaking engagement at a local chapter of a Women Presidents organization, and my session was from eighty-thirty to ten-thirty. Because it was so beautiful, I decided to walk over the Brooklyn Bridge into downtown Manhattan and up to my meeting, which was about fourteen blocks north of the World Trade Center, and I remember the blue sky and the sunshine on that morning.

I arrived around eight, set up, and greeted the participants for my session, which was on entrepreneurial leadership. At 8:46, I heard a loud crashing sound, which I thought must have been a truck accident. My back was to the windows and I turned around and looked up and saw that the first airplane had hit the towers.

In the room, some of the women knew people on those floors. We decided, as a group, to start calling family and friends. Then the second plane hit the towers. Panic started to set in. I knew that one of my clients was in those buildings filming a financial news program. The other participants were now shaking and crying. I left with two friends and we went to use the phone at one of their offices, which was toward the towers. People started running. The next thing I remember is a taxicab with its doors open.

The driver was staring up and the radio was blaring that the Pentagon had been hit. Up until that moment, I was not worried about our safety, but then my own panic set in and I started shutting down. What was happening? Was the whole Eastern seaboard under attack? We ran from Tribeca to my friend's home on 21st Street. I don't remember the towers falling.

That afternoon my husband came to get me and we took the long walk home through dark streets and blowing sheets of paper everywhere. For three days, lower Manhattan had no power and we had no television, Internet, or phone service because the transmitters had been on the top of the towers before they fell. It was like science fiction, and it was the view from my loft windows on the East River waterfront.

So what does this have to do with Alignment?

Partly from my own experience, I have an ongoing fascination with how people overcome adversity. I have spent many years attempting to understand what makes some people victims and others survivors of their difficult life experiences. I have interviewed people who have undergone terrible ordeals—from abuse to natural disaster to torture and imprisonment —and I have studied fear and bounce-back in individuals, teams, and organizations. I have viewed resilience through many lenses, from working with post-traumatic stress survivors, as a graduate student intern in clinical psychology, to working with the best and brightest organizational leaders as an executive leadership consultant and coach.

Because of that experience on September 11 of 2001, I was able to take my understanding of how organizations and individuals cope with trauma, loss, and change, and use it to positive ends through teaching organizational leaders and practitioners about trauma and bouncing back. I was drawn to cultivate new practices that reduced my fear and stress (and gave me back my joy and calm), and to learn as much as I could about what enables people to survive, and even thrive, under duress.

I learned something important personally—that my quality of life, my own healing, depended upon my putting my experience to use. I recognized that those people I saw who got into action as a response to their experience were instantly better off than those who didn't, and I saw that companies that acknowledged what had happened and addressed the reality of trauma were in much better shape than those that did not.

The same attributes that help us to overcome obstacles or traumas are the ones that make for incredible leaders who have long, enduring careers. Research by Linda Hoopes, Ph.D., President of The Resilience Alliance, on approximately seventy thousand people working primarily in the corporate sector, shows that those people who are elevated to more senior positions have greater levels of resilience. They are able to handle change more effectively, and may even select into their roles because they enjoy being challenged and adapting to change.

Resilient people are able to see the positive even in the most difficult of circumstances. It may not come naturally; it may be a discipline they choose. Linda Hoopes has this to say about her research: "Energy and drive to overcome obstacles come from seeing possibility and opportunities. If you don't have that then everything you do is about defending against dangers or potential losses".[17] In my own research with colleague Alan Graham, PhD, we've assessed thousands of executives with a tool we created called the Resilience at Work Assessment, and we've found that the number one attribute of people with overall high resilience is a sense of purpose. When we feel like we are part of something greater than just ourselves we are capable of handling the changes that come at us no matter what the circumstance.

Leadership Challenges and Alignment

We all have those experiences of crisis, challenge, and survival that we need to get through as leaders and as human beings. As I watch my clients cope with the effect of downsizing, resizing, and world-shifting change, I think focus on Alignment can be a great way to remember what strategies really work.

---

[17] Interview with Linda Hoopes, Ph.D., June 22, 2009

Fear-based behavior and fear-based decision-making can cripple a business. Organizations depend on their people's ability to get out of fear-based behavior because every company experiences setbacks. In particular, people within the organization look to their leaders for guidance, so leaders need to be able to understand and learn from what's happened and bring a positive vision of the future to their teams, no matter what the challenge. Great leaders acknowledge what is and help people see what can be.

Alignment helps us steer through the everyday stresses and hassles that fill modern life, and helps us bounce back from adverse events such as job loss, divorce, or a death in the family. We can become helpless and resigned to our fate or we can use our internal resources to bounce back. Alignment helps us reach out into the world and find renewed purpose and meaning in life. This allows us to achieve what we are capable of, both individually and organizationally.

In order to address challenges, we need to understand that we have a profound impact— and we need to know just how powerful we are. Each one of us is powerful beyond measure, and we have an impact on ourselves, our teams, and our whole organization.

Crisis Leadership: Keeping it Simple and Building Trust

Think of the leaders who are standing out at the beginning of the Covid-19 pandemic. Jacinda Ardern, Prime Minister of New Zealand and Andrew Cuomo, governor of New York are two leaders who are garnering great attention for their calm, steadfast and empathic approach to leading in a crisis. In fact, worldwide both of these leaders has a large following outside of their respective jurisdictions as people seek leadership during this moment of crisis. Each of them has their own unique style, but there are some clear similarities:

1. **"Keep Calm, Carry On" messaging**. Both Ardern and Cuomo are taking the shock value out of their communication by presenting facts, telling brief stories that demonstrate empathy, and asking their

constituents consistently in every communication to be patient and kind with each other.

2. **A 'Safety First' Focus.** Both Ardern and Cuomo have referred to their economic and health struggles from the perspective of safety and security—addressing people from that lowest level of Maslow's hierarchy of needs—survival.

3. **Humanizing Moments.** Cuomo has joked via video chat with his quarantined brother Chris and told stories about his mother. Ardern has gone on Facebook Live after putting her child to bed and told the children of New Zealand that the Easter Bunny is indeed an essential worker and will not be kept home.

4. **Acknowledging Economic Challenges.** Both Ardern and Cuomo have acknowledged the damage their respective shutdowns will do to their economies, but their messages are clear – we will address this health crisis as a road to addressing the economic one.

5. **Highlighting Collaboration.** Ardern and Cuomo have both built coalitions with health experts, heads of state, business community leaders, and others in order to a) view the crisis from multiple angles and b) create solutions through collaborative effort.

Levels of Alignment: The Three Circles of Impact

The three levels of Alignment begin with you at the center. They move to your immediate circle of influence—your team—and then on to your organization at the outer ring. At each level, you have the capacity for positive impact, but it all starts with you and your own commitment.

Level One: Individual Alignment

Individually, Alignment starts with empowerment. When we feel that we have personal power to impact our world for the better, to create change, we are equipped with a foundation for bouncing back from adversity and for meeting challenge with a belief that it is possible to grow. Individually, we believe in our ability to create a positive outcome no matter what the circumstance.

Crisis, challenge, and change were the themes of Susan Taylor's life when she was twenty-four years old. Here's how she used her Alignment to address those themes and to transform herself:

In 1970, Susan Taylor found herself separated, rent due, with a small child. "After the breakup of my first marriage, I realized it was my sole responsibility to feed, clothe, and educate my daughter. This…compelled me to live my life with purpose." One Sunday morning she went to the emergency room with pain in her chest and difficulty breathing. Her anxiety had gotten the better of her, and her doctor prescribed "relaxation".

Walking up Broadway in New York City, Taylor went into a church to sit down—and heard a sermon that inspired her, and ended up changing her life forever. "The preacher said that our minds could change our world. That no matter what our troubles, if we could put them aside for a moment, focus on possible solutions, and imagine a joyous future, we would find peace within, and positive experiences would begin to unfold." She decided to try it.

Susan's willingness to push forward, and to adopt a positive, can-do attitude, got her to the top of *Essence* magazine, eventually becoming editor-in-chief. She has been cited as "the most influential black woman in journalism today" by American Libraries. She is a bestselling author, a keynote speaker, and holds an honorary doctorate.

How did she get there?

She engaged her natural capacity for positivity, hard work, developing relationships and not letting anything stop her to achieve her own greatness and to impact her world for the better.

Alignment can protect us from being shattered by illness or overcome by difficult experiences. It is what enables us to take our experiences and make meaning out of them, and ultimately to transcend them through creating a new reality. We become powerful—rather than victims of our circumstances —and we take charge.

Level Two: Team Alignment

Building a team takes time and effort, and mostly a collective positive vision of what can be achieved together. Successful teams have the capacity to confront reality, learn from mistakes, and align around decisions. They have a "we," versus "me," attitude, and it shows in how they function as a unit. Because of the lack of blaming, individuals are comfortable taking responsibility for good and bad outcomes, admit failures, and work with their counterparts to develop and grow.

Successful teams are those who move through the phases of team development successfully—forming, storming, norming, and performing[23] —and keep working at it over time. They may have to repeat the cycle, but they get better at it every repetition.

They are able to shift gears because they have agreed to operate according to a set of working principles, and they know what to do when there is a change: get together, make decisions, and act based on an agreed-upon trajectory. They have the basics down: respect, commitment, and follow-through.

Let's take a real-world example of a team whose company name shall remain anonymous to protect the guilty. The head of a supply chain for a global organization was known to his team as a terrible, tyrannical boss who was constantly critical of his people. Let's call him Andrew. He was an analytical thinker who was proud of his outstanding results in improving

quality and performance in his last company. He liked to tell his team how excellent his former group was, and how they were "real thinkers," unlike the new team.

In order to build a team that could weather this storm and create a more positive future, Andrew had to take a hard look at his own behavior, and step back to think about how he could instill the attributes of resilience in his group. Because of his natural analytic ability, and with some gentle prodding from his consulting team, I might add, Andrew was able to start with a thorough assessment of the sabotaging, fear-based behaviors that were getting in their way.

He brought in facilitators to conduct a series of meetings that focused on clear, direct communication, alignment around decisions, and the benefit of developing positive attributes of Alignment, including adaptability, collaboration, and belief in a positive outcome.

The first step in reducing the fear?

Andrew had to step up and take responsibility for the blaming behaviors he'd been using, and demonstrate to the team that he was willing to trust the group. As a team, they have not only reduced their distracting, turf-based behaviors through focusing on their own strengths, they have turned around to become the absolute best in their business.

Team Alignment: Virtual Edition

Crisis leadership in a virtual environment means some important things for leadership and management.

1. **"Keep Calm, Carry On"**. Your people are looking to you as the voice of the organization and to let them know what to expect. If you don't know, be honest. The strongest leaders are able to say "We don't know, but we'll get through this together". When you have tough news to share, remember to re-orient people to the task at hand. "We've had to evacuate, but remember we're all for one, one for all."

1. **Keep yourself and your team healthy.** This doesn't just mean washing hands during a viral outbreak. This means pay attention to your team's psychological state and let them express their concerns to you. At times when there's great fear in organizations, people need more of your time and attention, not less.

2. **Remember this too shall pass.** There will be changes. Some things will look different later and we don't know exactly how. But as with all things, this too shall pass. Reminding your people that there is a future and a long-term view is powerful. They may be scared about this moment, but if you re-orient their thinking to the long term it can help shift fear into proactive and productive teamwork.

3. **Focus on the next most important thing.** Give simple messages about priorities. Have a vision of the future and take simple, clear action in the present. Make sure your team has a clear mandate of what is most important right now, and don't let them get too far ahead of this moment. It's easy for your people to get confused or

distracted during times of stress, particularly when they are in a virtual environment where distractions abound.

4. **If you know you will have layoffs, be honest.** One of the great fears your team may have is that they will lose their jobs. Tell them the truth. There are things you can and cannot control. "What we can control right now is doing a great job in order to contribute to the overall wellbeing of the company, of our clients, and of each other. If we get to the stage where we need to eliminate jobs, we'll let you know immediately."

5. **If illness directly impacts one of your team, be compassionate.** If you know that one of your team has a sick family member or is sick themselves give them an open door to tell you about it. It's a time to help people transcend their fear by giving them a sense of purpose, community, and hope. Let them know that you are there for them as a sounding board and to help problem solve if they need to take time off or get coverage for their role.

6. **Communicate more than usual.** People need to hear from their leaders during times of change, and when you're not in the same place it's easier for them to feel disconnected. This might mean having a quick daily check in with your team or reaching out directly to each of your team members individually over the course of a week. Notice who is doing well and who needs more of your focus. Provide them with tools and tips for working together.

Level Three: Organizational Alignment

Remember, Alignment is confidence in our ability to create a positive outcome no matter what the circumstance. Organizations that engage this belief have strength of purpose. They transcend the ordinary profit-making machines that make up much of modern business with a drive to make the world better. They accept what is and focus on the future, they build relationships and community, they view challenges as opportunities, and they practice discipline.

Those organizations that survive deep crisis are the ones that can address each level of Maslow's Hierarchy from survival (ensuring their financial security) to belonging (addressing the full employee lifecycle and culture effectively) to contribution (making a positive impact on customers) to transcendence (engaging in a higher purpose).

David Ryan, Managing Partner of ACE, an Australia based consulting firm, and co-author of the Business Acumen Gauge assessment and a forthcoming book on Business Acumen, has been focusing on Duty of Care as a core capability of strategic leadership for most of his eclectic leadership career. From working in the Ambulance Service as an intensive care paramedic to being an executive responsible for emergency operations the Ambulance Service, then serving as a senior executive for multiple industries, serving on boards and as a strategic advisor to CEOs and business owners, David has set out to research the core capabilities of leaders who get things done and done well.

According to Ryan "Duty of Care represents the alignment of the organizational values and its activities in delivering on its' purpose, whether for commercial or for not for profit organizations. Taking into consideration community, legislative, and stakeholder needs and expectations of ethical business practices is a primary duty of senior leadership. Duty of care is protecting the safety of workers, both physical and mental wellbeing. It also means contributing to the larger community that the organization serves, as well as the community it operates in."

"Examples of Duty of Care could include the Lemon act in the United States, which is a legislated form of Duty of Care, so the organization needs to take Duty of Care seriously in order to fulfill their brand promise and meet the needs of consumers so they don't walk away with a product that doesn't work. It could also be as fundamental as providing healthcare to your workforce or safety helmets and gear to a construction team." Duty of Care means we're aligning our organizational objectives to ethical leadership including values and mission.

Arie de Geus, formerly Shell's head of strategic planning, looked carefully at research done during a 1983 study of twenty-seven long-lived organizations to see how they thrived over time.[18] He found some critical similarities in those companies that survived over the long term:

- Using clearly stated values and missions to guide strategic decisions

- Learning and experimentation are part of the culture of the organization

- Excelling at seeing the future—experimenting at the margins of their markets and spotting trends and opportunities before they become threats

In order to survive over the long term, organizations must engage in Alignment. Alignment enables us to be guided by values and mission, it supports an attitude of learning and experimentation, and it enables looking to the future rather than just reacting to the present.

Part of organizational "bounce-back" ability is dependent on external factors, such as economy and competition. It is dependent on robust and adaptive strategies that takes into account what is happening not just with customers, but with the larger systems of government regulations, trade agreements, cultural realities, and global challenges of the future. Finally, it comes down to the people who populate the organization and how they engage and energize in order to execute that organization's promise.

Organizations that deal well with adversity or change have the ability to shift with the times—to be the right organization for what their customers need. During the Covid-19 global pandemic, we see companies pivoting to meet the needs of customers. In my own discipline - which is leadership consulting - I've seen competitive companies lose their footing and go under within six weeks of the pandemic due to their client's inability to pay, and their dependence on immediate cashflow. So how do we protect ourselves from this type of crisis?

---

[18] Arie de Geus, *The Living Company*

In order to weather a storm there are four areas of core strength that many big companies have that small businesses do not.

They are: strong and healthy coffers of capital, contingency plans/planning departments, robust digital infrastructure, and relationships with financial institutions.

In my own organization, we had been putting off a strategy to convert much of our training and development content, directed at senior executives, to online learning for a larger audience. All of a sudden, we realized as a team, that things were about to change and it was time to shift quickly.

We launched an app targeting a much larger audience than our typical elite executive coaching clients. Within four weeks of our own realization that the pandemic would reach us, and hit us hard, we had a clear path forward. That digital pivot made it possible for us to keep our core business moving while focusing on new audiences, innovation and delivering in new ways that customers needed immediately.

In a time of uncertainty, it's those organizations that cultivate clarity of purpose who are able to rally around that positive core and give their people a reason to push forward. Now, and in the future, successful organizations will be places that transcend the "profit for profit's sake" world of Milton Friedman economics. They will be places of greater purpose, filling the needs of a new breed of conscious consumers and employees. And they practice discipline by measuring their results—not just the bottom line.

Companies worldwide are measuring their success in a new way—their impact on people, planet, and profit. That triple-bottom-line reporting is an enormous change from profit-focus to the view that our organizations need to have a positive impact not just for their shareholders, but for their employees, their customers, their communities, and their environment.

Truly great organizations will be places of enlightenment and contribution for their employees. They will be places of meaning. Their employees will not be mired in fear-based behaviors like gossip, backstabbing, angry outbursts, punishment, and posturing. Their employees will be focused on collaboration and innovation—and getting things done in accordance with a greater purpose or mission.

As a next step, we need to acknowledge all of the benefits we get from staying in a state of fear, and we need to ask the question: If it's actually very simple to shift our state of being to one of Alignment, why are we so wedded to our fears?

Chapter 6

What Our Organizations (and Leaders) Gain from Living in Fear

"When you get to the end of your rope, tie a knot and hang on."

—Franklin D. Roosevelt

How do we change our systems to operate from Alignment not fear? We have to start with what is blocking our organizations from operating from creativity, openness, joy, and permission to deliver the best of ourselves.

Fight, flight, and freeze look different in organizations than in individuals, but the principles still hold.

Survival instincts are useful when a company is in a fight to do just that. Fear based behaviors are protective and of primary importance when there is a short-term crisis that threatens the life of that organization.

There is a very important role for fear during these moments as they help us to get down to basics. What costs can be cut? How can we contract and focus on the most important aspects of what we do and how we stay afloat? These are the positive elements of a rational and thoughtful fear response.

However, if we enter fight, flight, or freeze—the trauma response to fear—there can be dire consequences.

Organizational fight behavior might mean focusing too much on external competitors, and not enough on internal opportunities. Fear-based behaviors may take over your teams and arguing, escalating, and defensiveness become the main modes of communication. If you've ever seen a leadership team fighting, you know that it can be truly ugly. Territoriality, self-gain, posturing, and diminishing can sabotage an executive team, and the effectiveness of the organization at large.

Flight might mean opting out of something important in the future of the business, like shutting down expansion into new markets, launching new products, or acknowledging future trends.

Freezing organizationally means stopping the wheels of forward motion. I have seen leaders go into paralysis around decisions because they are waiting for more information. They stop looking at the future and what they want to create, and start focusing on what is wrong, to their own detriment.

If we get down to it, most of our blocks truly come from fear and from incentives to do things we know are wrong in the long term. There are five major fears that affect organizational leaders:

- Fear of collapse and destruction (losing it all if the company doesn't survive)

- Fear of failure (failing everyone, humiliation, being found out as a fraud, losing instead of winning)

- Fear of punishment (litigation, being left holding the bag)

- Fear of losing one's self (not living our purpose or contributing our best)

- Fear of losing one's job (being ousted or replaced)

What do these fears look like in action? I witnessed a famous CEO who shall remain nameless make a speech in front of their team: "I have no idea why this company would say we have a culture of fear. There should be no fear here". At the same time, they required everyone to sign a draconian confidentiality agreement that barred them from disclosing anything about their experience in the company to the outside world.

We need to focus on reducing fear on a large scale; we need to integrate Alignment into our workplace cultures and support it as it grows.

Remember, what we focus on becomes reality, and we want to stop focusing on fear.

Here's a story of how a culture of fear can throw off even the most talented and committed of leaders. The U.S. president of a major multinational company, we'll call him Deepak, was operating in a state of fear. Deepak was perceived in his initial years in the organization as having a strong moral compass. He had a reputation for integrity and for thinking through ideas on behalf of multiple stakeholders. He was well liked, a strong leader, and people wanted to work for him. He developed a loyal team of creative talent and through turbulent times, he kept on course.

This year was different.

Global leadership, who had a hands-off, distant relationship to the U.S. company, started piling new initiatives onto Deepak. Deepak kept responding to every possible initiative, afraid to say no. Meanwhile, people were feeling like failures because they couldn't get enough done on any project, let alone the new ones. Deepak was afraid to push back and stop the madness of new acquisitions, new initiatives, new strategies. Instead of saying no or reporting on the problems that resulted from taking on too much, he ended up putting on a happy face to senior leadership, while more and more was falling apart.

Deepak started questioning decisions that were being made, down to the minuscule and up to large strategy decisions. Whoever was last in his office was influencing the decision. The team was getting exhausted by seemingly random changes in focus and direction.

Deepak protected his own positional capital in the organization by siding with management despite his divergent beliefs. He began firing people who challenged him to stand up for his beliefs. From that day on, the people reporting directly to Deepak felt unsafe, fearful that they might be next on the chopping block. People lost trust in Deepak and in all of the leadership in the organization. People started to hang back rather than speak up. No one wanted to say anything confrontational, let alone creative or innovative, in case Deepak's bosses didn't like it, and Deepak caved to their desires. Once the leader starts to question people openly and speak negatively about people in the organization, the rest of the team follows suit.

Deepak started out confident when he was hired into the organization. Through years of developing greater and greater fear of letting people down, not being liked, and being ejected from the group, Deepak lost that confidence and his credibility. He began to doubt his own values, ethics, and competence. The very best people started to leave because good people wouldn't put up with it. There was a failure script that had started to play in the organization, which became more and more self-reinforcing.

How did Deepak get to the place where he made the decision to start throwing people under the bus, sacrificing his own people, getting out of integrity, and blowing the sense of trust he'd built with his team? How did he start giving up his own leadership power?

A corporate culture of fear had trained people to maximize self-preservation. Deepak was not predisposed to behave that way, but the training was insidious and very effective. Deepak's story is a cautionary tale. Once we start acting based on fear and going against our own beliefs, our credibility is shot and we start going down a slippery slope.

So how do we change a whole system and encourage healthier ways of working? First, we have to accept what is—that there are rewards for organizations and leaders living in fear-based behavior.

Gain #1: Short Term-ism

Short-termism is valuable in a crisis, because it shifts us into getting through this present moment and surviving to fight another day. However, when we stay in short-termism forever it sabotages our long-term gains.

So many of us are compensated on short-term wins. When we are tempted to line our own pockets and those of our team members for short-term gain, we may benefit personally, but what about the impact on the business and on society as a whole? We are afraid to look to the long term because our systems are set up to deliver us rewards for short-term thinking.

Continuously focusing on quarterly earnings versus long-term survival is the number one killer of sustainable, healthy businesses. We need to operate from Alignment in order to turn this one around. It's time for us to wake up to what short-term thinking really achieves.

Every public company faces the pressure of short-term thinking and short-term shareholder return. The good news? Leaders, shareholders, consumers, and employees are all becoming savvier and more proactive about wanting to shift focus to long-term sustainability and long-term value.

Jeff Bezos is currently the richest person on earth in 2020. What got him there? Well, it wasn't focusing on the short term! Jeff Bezos stated in an interview in 2000, "Every minute spent thinking about the short-term stock price is a minute wasted". What was happening with Amazon in 2000? They were in a stock price nosedive of 80% during the first dotcom bubble bursting, but Bezos was sticking to what he told shareholders early on in 1997; it's all about the long term. Instead of reacting in fight, flight, or freeze, Bezos made decisions betting on his long-term vision that over 15% of commerce would move online (at that time, e-commerce represented less than 1% of retail sales). That year, he solidified his approach that Amazon.com would be run with a long-term view versus a focus on short term gains. That long-term orientation reduced the impact of stock price fluctuations on strategic decision making.

In 2019, in the United States, the Long-Term Stock Exchange became the 14th (and latest) stock exchange. The Long-Term Stock Exchange requires all participating companies to set governance standards and incentives that reward long-term thinking and strategies that focus on longer time horizons.

Companies can raise capital based on long term strategy versus short-term gain.

Eric Ries, author and creator of The Lean Startup methodology, and CEO of the Long-Term Stock Exchange asked a powerful question: Why are we doing things this way? The answer is: **when we change the way incentives work, we can remake our systems in smarter ways.**

After Enron's demise from accounting fraud in 2003, The Aspen Institute, a sixty-year-old non-profit dedicated to fostering values-based leadership and providing a neutral venue for discussing and acting upon critical issues, created its Corporate Values Strategy Group "to re-evaluate business practices leading to malfeasance and short-sighted decision making in business".

The Aspen Institute issued a report in 2010 entitled *"Long-Term Value Creation: Guiding Principles for Corporations and Investors,"* in which they call for companies and investors to de-emphasize short-term metrics and instead "maximize future value (even at the expense of lower near-term earnings) and to provide the investment community and other key stakeholders the information they need to make better decisions about long-term value". The Aspen Institute's recommendations are no small indicator of change.

According to a study by the Conference Board, pressure to meet short-term quarterly earnings numbers can cause market volatility and can cause management to lose sight of its strategic business model. Well, yeah! Anyone who works in a major public company has seen short-term thinking sabotage long-term thinking at some point. If corporations, investors and financial analysts begin to reorient, we have much to gain. Not only does long-term thinking enhance our ability to maintain stable financial markets, it comes down to basic, primal survival.

Short term-ism can mean shifting capital needed for business survival and growth over the long term. The temptation to drive for short-term trading profits can drive investors (institutional and otherwise) to pressure company executives to make decisions that hurt the organization's long-term prospects. Our economies lose because companies that are not investing in long-term growth aren't innovating, and they may eventually lose steam, plateau, or fail.

Let's take a very simple example of longer-term thinking.

An enthusiastic young worker in a small company started a Sustainability Task Force. The task force came up with a set of recommendations to leadership, and the rule was that each recommendation needed to pay for itself over time, or be a net financial gain for the company.

The first idea was a one-hundred-thousand-dollar retrofit on an existing facility. The payout would take seven years but would come back in money saved on utilities.

The second idea was to replace existing light bulbs with fluorescents, the cost savings coming back within two years.

These two seemingly small investments had a proven return but they were not palatable to the organization, which wanted to put their capital investments into something more traditional: redecorating the executive suite and client entertainment area.

What was the outcome of the organization saying no to these longer-term ideas? The task force disbanded, some enthusiastic young talent was disappointed and started looking elsewhere for employment, and the organization got more of the same, rather than a new infusion of purpose, energy, and engagement.

TRY THIS

Getting out of Short-Term Thinking: The Ten-Percent Solution

We all get into the rut of addressing day-to-day issues without having time to focus on the long term. If we took ten percent of our own (and our team's) time to focus on the long term, what would come from it?

Step One: Set aside four hours of your work week to focus on long-term activities.

Step Two: Evaluate after one month. What changes did you make? What happened as a result of that shift in priorities?

Gain #2: Staying Alert and Prepared for Crisis

Fear can be a way to remain vigilant. As a result, we are alert and prepared. But we need not be overcome by fear of the future as long as we acknowledge the real.

What's the difference between a challenge and a crisis? A crisis is a threat to the immediate survival of the organization, or to the immediate health and well-being of people associated with it.

During a crisis, we may need some fear. That fear is informative. As long as it isn't the kind of fear that locks us down into fight, flight, or freeze without the ability to make conscious choices, it's good information. The key is to stay alert, be prepared, and be informed by our fear rather than controlled by it.

Here's a short list of a few of the crisis situations that might at some point affect you and your organization:

- Workplace violence

- Natural disaster

- Product recall

- Criminal investigation

- Hostile takeover

- Terrorist attack

- Class-action lawsuit

- Internet hacking

- Insider trading

- Death of key executives

- Supply chain disruptions

- Economic collapse

According to Jim Moorhead, Senior Director, Crisis Management and Litigation Communication, at APCO Worldwide, the sharpest companies have their radar up all the time:

> The first thing they do is to conduct a vulnerability audit and identify potential threats either internal or external. For example, it could come from the outside world—a hostile takeover, a regulatory investigation, a shareholder class action—or it could come from the internal world—a sexual harassment claim against an executive, a manufacturing problem. Companies that look at the landscape of risk try to identify and rank what is most likely and what needs attention paid to it. The third part of the vulnerability audit is to take specific threats in detail and look at people responsible for each area, and what can be done to improve our capabilities to respond to those threats.

Some crisis situations that require a healthy dose of fear are those in which a company's character is under assault. Those can be life-threatening. During the Covid-19 global pandemic, the aforementioned Amazon.com's reputation is wavering as stories come out about not providing employees protective gear, enough space, and lack of transparency about exposure to the virus.

In early 2009, two Domino's employees filming themselves preparing pizza and sandwiches that included putting food up their noses and, worse, posting this video on YouTube. It got a million hits and attracted a firestorm of online discussions.

These crisis situations involve basic questions: What happened? What are you doing about it? How do we know it won't happen again? The company had a decision to make. Would they acknowledge it or not? A couple of days after the video, the Domino's CEO did a straight-to-the-camera apology and expressed outrage about their tampering with the food supply, which is a criminal offense.

Smart organizations don't let crises put them into fight, flight, or freeze. They have a plan, and they are prepared to act on that plan.

TRY THIS
Identify Issues for Scenario Planning

This particular exercise is designed to make your dialog valuable as you address different arenas that impact your business. It is adapted from Peter Schwartz, who wrote in artful detail about scenario planning in the highly recommended book *The Art of the Long View*. This is one that requires a facilitator who is not on your team, and who has experience with strategic planning.

STEP ONE: Identify What's Keeping You Awake at Night

Take a few minutes to jot down some of the critical decisions facing your company or organization. Review and discuss; choose one or two ideas to serve as the focal issue for your scenarios.

STEP TWO: Environmental Scan

Take a look at the macro: What world changes are impacting your business? Hang up separate flip charts for each topic area and take a full hour to write up a scan of the following areas:

1. ENVIRONMENT

2. HEALTH

3. SOCIAL NORMS/CULTURE

4. POLITICS

5. TECHNOLOGY

6. ECONOMY

7. RESOURCE AVAILABILITY

8. COMPETITION

STEP THREE: Do a Gallery Walk

Have each person in your group review what is on the flip charts. Discuss trends you see.

STEP FOUR: Rank Issues by Importance and Uncertainty

Rank the top issues you see, using the categories of *importance* and *uncertainty*.

You are looking for the issues that are the most important, and the most uncertain. These two headlines will give you great insights into what you need to address in scenario planning.

There may only be one driving force that seems both critical and uncertain—or there may be two or three. Choosing more than three for discussion gets cumbersome.

STEP FIVE: Create Scenarios/Create Your Plan

Once you have your top issues by importance and uncertainty, you can create one, two, or even three scenarios to work through as a group. The scenario might be very simple; if you were working at an airline, it might be an airplane crash scenario. The plan would address the top issues posed by that scenario.

STEP SIX: Scenario Plan Must-Haves

Make sure your plan addresses the what, who, how, and when that will happen based on your issue. The plan needs to include what each department does to address the issue—from PR/communications (and what the executives would be expected to say), to training and development, and HR (how do the flight attendants respond, how do customer service reps handle inquiries, what do they do to contact loved ones?), to technology, to engineering and maintenance. Each area of the business must be prepared to either avoid or handle these scenarios.

Remember, these exercises take time, and you may need multiple days to address these issues.

Gain #3: Denial and Discounting the Future

When is denial a gain? When it protects us from having to face the awful truth. Denial is adaptive and can keep us in a positive frame of mind. The problem? That time is fleeting while the world passes you by! An organization that believes that things will stay the same, or that they have plenty of time to make incremental changes, is dead wrong—and unprepared. The CDC, the World Health Organization, and the Bill and Melinda Gates foundation consistently warned of the dangers of an upcoming global pandemic to our global society, but many of us have been in denial about the level of impact it might have on us or our businesses.

As change gets more rapid, and we know that's happening because the speed of technology is revving up exponentially, we see more symptoms of future shock—including denial.

Currently, we can look at country by country responses to the novel coronavirus and the drastic difference between those who were prepared and those who were not. Specifically, some Asian countries had dealt with epidemics before and used that experience to develop strategies. Taiwan's response—hailed by CNN as one of the best in the world— was defined by their experience because they were hit worst by SARS.

"Taiwan is in such a strong position now that, after weeks of banning the export of face masks to ensure domestic supply, the government said that it would donate 10 million masks to the United States, Italy, Spain and nine other European countries, as well as smaller nations who have diplomatic ties with the island," according to James Griffiths of CNN.com. [19] What was the right approach according to Taiwanese leadership? Strong decisive action included ramping up face mask production and ensuring local supply, banning travel early and fully, enacting home quarantine, and communicating with transparency so citizens were informed. What can we learn about crisis leadership from Taiwanese preparedness, messaging, and action?

------

[19] Griffiths, James, *Taiwan's Response to Coronavirus is Among the Best Globally*, CNN.com April 5, 2020

112

1. **Learn from experience.** Taiwan used the experiences of their past to inform their plans for the future.

2. **Conserve resources as needed.** Securing protective face masks at the beginning of the crisis helped Taiwan to be in a strong position. In fact, Taiwan plans on donating over ten million masks to the United States, Spain, Italy and others.

3. **Take swift and decisive action.** From securing face masks to shutting down borders, Taiwan made decisions as early as January 2020, when other countries were not yet acknowledging the threat from Wuhan.

4. **Commit to transparent communication.** Much like other leaders we've mentioned like Cuomo and Ardern, Taiwan's President Tsai Ing-wen has been clear and communicative with her people, creating a sense of public trust in authority.

5. **Build relationships and community.** Politics with China aside, by exporting personal protective equipment, Taiwan is solidifying positive relationships with global allies that may prove useful in the future.

One famous case study is an organization that failed to get out of denial and adapt to the changing needs of their customers; Kodak. It was an organization with an incredible brand; everyone wanted Kodak film. If you were doing anything innovative, you went to Kodak. They saw digital coming down the path, but they resisted that new change in technology, even though they saw that it was revolutionizing the photography industry—and they even helped develop it! Instead, their strategy was completely geared toward selling more film. Unwillingness to change—to be in denial—can kill a company.

Kodak could've been an early innovator but they slowed down development in order to protect and preserve their dominance in print. They are still fighting their way back into brand dominance because of their denial that their industry was changing faster than they were.

The music industry was famously slow to catch on to single unit downloads and streaming models, damaging their ability to capitalize on new technologies. How is your company denying the rapid changes coming to your industry sector?

TRY THIS

Seeing Future Disruptions

When assessing the landscape for strengths, weaknesses, opportunities, and challenges, we sometimes miss disruptive technologies or social changes that will rapidly change our business landscape.

- What are the disruptions in your industry that you need to watch for?

- What have you been denying as an organization?

- What strategy do you have in place now that will get you through rapid, disruptive change?

Gain #4: Getting People to Jump When You Say "Jump"

Some leaders love the feeling of power they get when employees fear them.

Managing based on fear was the strategy of the CEO of a major media company that went from a billion-dollar company (with shares selling for over thirty dollars) to having exponentially lost value when it was recently sold at almost twenty cents per share. We'll call him Doug.

Doug didn't value his most valuable asset—his executive team—when he came into the company as a new leader. He wanted to keep control at the top, so he didn't share information and his philosophy was about "keeping people on their toes". He created an atmosphere of fear. His controlling behavior extended into refusing to collaborate or partner with employees.

Doug would say to his team, "We need to own the space. We need to control our relationships". The message to the group, who had created a strategy based on building partnerships, was that they were wrong. Executives started to defect. The share price began to sink. While it wasn't just Doug's "motivate by fear" leadership style that landed them there, it was a definite contributor.

Think about this. According to a study performed by the Saratoga Institute, the number of employers who believe their people leave for more money is 89 percent. The actual number of people who leave for a higher pay check? Twelve percent. They're not leaving for the money; they're leaving because they don't have positive relationships with their managers, they don't feel respected, and they don't feel as though they are valued. **When we lead based on fear rather than on engagement, we lose the best people and we get the worst of the rest.**

Gallup statistics show that disengaged workers cost the American business economy up to three hundred and fifty billion dollars annually in lost productivity. What a waste!

Gain#5: Holding On To What Is Without Allowing the Dream of What Could Be

Real resilience, real adaptability, would mean that we were flexible and adaptable enough to create a truly sustainable world. It would mean seeing that the natural adaptive cycle might mean death of one system in order to create room for the new.

A truly resilient organization is one that does not hold on to the idea that the current structure is the right one—even the structures that exist in society that determine what the concept of organization means.

Some claim that the longest living corporation is Stora Kopparberg. It is thought to have been started prior to the issuance of its first share in 1288. In its first incarnation, it was a copper-mining company and was officially chartered by King Magnus IV of Sweden in 1347. Toward the end of the 1800s, Stora diversified and moved into paper production. By the 1960s, Stora Kopparberg Bergslags Aktiebolag was Sweden's largest producer of electricity, dairy, produce, steel, and industrial chemicals. Now Stora-Enso (Stora merged with a Finnish paper company) is the second largest paper producer in the world. What Stora has managed to do is to continuously grow, diversify, change, and manage efficiencies. They never got in the trap of identifying with one product.[20]

If we truly believe that this is a time of a great correction—a truing of accounts, so to speak—and that our finite global system requires us to make a giant leap forward in replenishing our natural resources, reinvigorating our ecosystems, providing for the vast number of people without access to food, clean water, and sanitary living conditions, reducing violence, and building quality of life for living beings of all kinds, then we may need to rethink how we work and what purpose our organizations serve.

We have the power to dream, to imagine, and to create anew. Don't underestimate the power of a dream! New creation comes from our ability to imagine. Famous dreamer Thomas Edison had to fail many times before achieving his dream, but it happened and our modern world is filled with electric light. How do we engage in a new dream—allowing ourselves to dream what could be—and to work toward that?

We can take our cues from some unlikely sources.

---

20 "The Oldest Corporation in the World," *Time Magazine*, Friday March 15, 1963

Linda Curtis is a powerful businesswoman and a leader in financial services. She has held officer and vice president positions at U.S. Bancorp and The Harris Bank of Chicago and, during her tenure at Visa USA, she led an award-winning business development team, negotiating multi-million-dollar agreements with Fortune 500 companies such as AT&T, AOL Time Warner, and State Farm Insurance.

Linda Curtis was working at Visa in San Francisco, California, when she was invited by a friend to attend a luncheon and stumbled upon a not-for-profit organization that blew her circuits—and got her dreaming a new dream. That organization is the Pachamama Alliance, a group that works with the indigenous Achuar people of the Ecuadorian Amazon to bridge the modern and ancient worlds. Their belief is that we have a great deal to learn from each other, and that the Achuar can give us a new perspective on dreaming what could be.

Just a few months later, Linda was in the Amazon rainforest experiencing viscerally what it was to be part of nature, inextricably dependent on other people for survival, and dependent upon the rainforest for sustenance. She learned that the Achuar are a dream-based culture that trusts their dreams to help them survive as a community.

In dreams, they were told that they would not survive unless they partnered with the modern world. Through those dreams, together with a stalwart group of people from the modern North, they have created a viable way to survive without taking money from oil companies and without sacrificing their land. They have built and now manage an eco-lodge in the rainforest, and have their own small fleet of planes to fly people into the jungle.

The Achuar legend is a prophecy that's been passed down through the generations, going back hundreds and possibly thousands of years, from the Andean region of South America. It is said that at this time, the world would be dominated by the eagle people, the people of the global North, the people of the mind, the intellect, and technology. They would dominate the condor people.

The condor people are represented by the indigenous people, the people who have a connection to their hearts, to the earth, and to the more subtle realms of our existence. This cycle would last for five hundred years—that's how they count time in the Andes, through five-hundred-year cycles. The last five hundred-year cycle began at the end of the 1400s, right around the time of Columbus, so it ushered in this time of conquest over indigenous people, over nature, and even over our own hearts.

It was said that the people of the North, the eagle people, would reach a zenith in their capacity to build technology, but they would become, in a way, spiritually impoverished to such an extent that it would threaten their very existence.

The people of the South, the condor people, would become very evolved in their spiritual understanding of humanity and nature, but they would become materially impoverished to such an extent that their existence would be threatened. At this point in history, there would be a shift in this cycle of time and the eagle and the condor would remember that they are connected, and they would fly together in the same sky, wing to wing.

We would understand that we are interdependent, that the condor people need the gifts that the eagle people have, the gifts of the mind and the intellect, and the eagle people would need the gifts that the condor people have to offer, and that's the understanding of spirit and the understanding of nature and sustainability.

It's prophesied that the earth will come into balance as these two people represented by the birds, the eagle and the condor, fly together in the same sky, wing to wing, bringing the earth into balance.

Instead of responding to the modern world with fear, the Achuar listened to their dreams and responded with Alignment—the confidence to create a new, more positive future together. We have much to learn from their acceptance of what is, focus on the future, building of relationships and community, seeing challenge as opportunity, and practice of discipline.

TRY THIS

Remember You Are Part of the Natural World

Getting yourself or your team out of the office and into nature can change your perspective in profound and unexpected ways. You don't have to go to the Amazon to experience raw, pristine nature. Do your homework and find the spot closest to you with undeveloped, natural terrain. Make the attempt to find someplace that is not a park or city garden, but somewhere that has been preserved in its wild, natural essence.

Take this book or your own journal and go on retreat for at least one full day. Take a break from your cell phones and your email. Take time for contemplation. Listen to your hidden, innermost thoughts. What new ideas or dreams come to you when you retreat into the wilderness? What insights do you gain through disconnecting from the rushed pace of your workplace? If you have trouble letting go of whatever your to-do list might be, make sure to take time to write it down, delegate what you can, and let go of the rest temporarily so you can truly get the benefit of disconnecting.

Alignment is the only state that can truly liberate us from staying stuck in our current reality and move us toward a new, constructive beginning.

When living in Alignment, we are not swayed by beliefs like "it can't be changed" or "that's not possible". We replace those beliefs with "We will find our way together". Our next chapter will focus on how to get your team into Alignment.

Chapter 7

Organizational Alignment:
Activating Your Team

"Coming together is a beginning. Keeping together is progress. Working together is success."

—Henry Ford

A Team Story

One story of a team going into truly uncharted territory and prevailing despite great challenges is that of the Apollo 11 mission to the moon. The Apollo 11 crew, led by Mission Commander Neil Armstrong, Lunar Module Pilot Edwin "Buzz" Aldrin, and Command Module Pilot Michael Collins, had some challenges that could easily have stopped the successful moon landing of July 20, 1969, or perhaps their safe return.

It took many people to make this first moon landing possible: from the vision of John Kennedy saying famously, "I believe that this nation should commit itself to achieving the goal, before this decade is out, of landing a man on the Moon and returning him safely to the Earth," to the scientists who created the instrumentation, the suits they wore, the spacecraft, the propulsion engines, the flight directors who guided their mission from Earth, and the backup crew, there were many people on the Apollo 11 team besides the three astronauts.

On July 19, mission control gave the go-ahead for the Apollo 11 to make its historic descent to the moon's surface from orbit.

Right at the time the engines started they lost data communications, which then picked back up. Two minutes into the descent, Armstrong noticed they were off course. He said, "We're gonna be a little long," and noted that they were off of their targeted landing site. Then the alarms started—codes

121

being sent to the computer at mission control. The computer was overloaded with radar information from two sources and it couldn't process all of the data. They did a software restart. Armstrong and Aldrin took over in a "semi-manual" landing, where they maneuvered the spacecraft to scoot along the moon's surface and find a boulder-free place to land.

THEN the fuel light went on. They had been using extra fuel in finding a new landing site. They only had one hundred and twenty seconds of margin. The crew at mission control was glued to their monitors. When Armstrong came on the audio and said, "The Eagle has landed," the ground crew burst into applause and cheers.

After landing on the moon, preparation to leave the capsule took over two hours. Some of the highest heart rates recorded from the astronauts were during entry and exit, and wouldn't you know it, they forgot to change the design of the life support backpacks when they made the hatch smaller—oops! Squeezing through the hatch was an ordeal, but they got through, posed on the moon for photographs, and set up a television transmission before beginning the hard work of gathering samples in low gravity.

After this momentous first walk on another world, the tired astronauts climbed back into the hatch, tossed out many of their heavier items, and Aldrin, moving about the cabin, accidentally broke the circuit breaker that armed the main engine for lift off. At first, they thought they might not be able to arm the engine. Using a felt-tip pen, they were able to activate the switch. After seven hours of much-needed sleep, they launched the Eagle and got back to the Saturn V, returning home to earth.

How did the astronauts deal with the tremendous stressors and unknowns? First, they accepted each reality as it happened and focused on what to do next. They viewed every challenge as temporary, as one more opportunity to succeed. They had strong relationships of trust with their ground crew and each other, and they never broke down into blaming and arguing; they acted as a unit and achieved greatness together. The three astronauts—as a team—faced their situation with Alignment.

Here are the words of Collins, Aldrin, and Armstrong on the last night before their return:

> Collins commented that he was absolutely confident that the Saturn V rocket would work because of the power of the team. "All this is possible only through the blood, sweat, and tears of a number of a people... All you see is the three of us, but beneath the surface are thousands and thousands of others, and to all of those, I would like to say, "Thank you very much".

> Aldrin wanted people everywhere to feel the awe that he felt during this experience, and the expansiveness of the connection of people throughout this great endeavor. "This has been far more than three men on a mission to the Moon; more, still, than the efforts of a government and industry team; more, even, than the efforts of one nation."

> Armstrong concluded, "The responsibility for this flight lies first with history and with the giants of science who have preceded this effort; next with the American people, who have, through their will, indicated their desire; next with four administrations and their Congresses, for implementing that will; and, then, with the agency and industry teams that built our spacecraft, the Saturn, the Columbia, the Eagle, and the little EMU, the spacesuit and backpack that was our small spacecraft out on the lunar surface. We would like to give special thanks to all those Americans who built the spacecraft; who did the construction, design, the tests, and put their hearts and all their abilities into those craft. To those people tonight, we give a special thank you, and to all the other people that are listening and watching tonight, God bless you. Good night from Apollo 11".[21]

---

[21] http://science.ksc.nasa.gov/history/apollo/apollo-11/apollo-11.html

Leading a Team: Applying the Four Practices

The astronauts used it...and the best teamwork comes from using these same four practices:

- Accepting what is, and focusing on the future

- Building relationships and community

- Viewing challenges as opportunities

- Practicing physical and mental discipline

Alignment Practice #1: Accepting What Is and Focusing on the Future

The most resilient teams are the ones that "confront the brutal facts," as Jim Collins would say, and remove blame. Instead of being stopped in our tracks when there's been a breakdown, a resilient team is able to discuss whatever mistakes they've made, within the framework of the principles of Alignment. This sounds simple, but many teams that don't have a structure for learning will sweep problems under the rug, ignore what's broken down, and blame each other—rather than learn. No learning can happen when the debriefing is done from judgement. A professional sports team, for example, wouldn't look at the game they lost and blame it on one person. Every pro-sport team will look at the game and say what they did well, and what can they learn. This practice is no different for any other environment. Instead of pointing fingers, a resilient team takes a non-judgmental stance and uses the lessons learned from the practices of alignment to create a more resilient team.

TRY THIS

Team Exercise: Lessons Learned Session

"Our greatest glory is not in never falling, but in rising every time we fall."

—Confucius

Team Ground Rules

For this exercise, a set of upfront rules of engagement sets the stage for success.

Suggested ground rules might be:

1. Assume best intentions.

2. Respect time boundaries; focus without interruption until breaks.

3. Bring it all to the table, no matter how messy.

4. End with solutions, not blame.

5. Agree that what's past is past, and that its value is in the lessons we can learn from it to move forward.

Instructions: Lessons Learned Session

1. As a team, choose a period of time to review: one month, one quarter, one year.

2. Brainstorm a list of what happened over that period of time and break it into two columns: on the right, write the facts; on the left, write the interpretations of the team.

3. Identify the areas of agreement and disagreement.

4. Identify lessons to be learned from the experience of that time period.

5. Wrap up with a list of actions to be taken based on lessons learned.

A.   Simplify and Clarify

It's easier said than done to do a great job prioritizing when there's a great deal to do—particularly when senior management wants everything done yesterday, fast, under budget, and with fewer resources than normal.

The truth is, we are having to make tough decisions, and most organizational leaders are being pressured to do the impossible, which is everything. We have a superhero myth that makes us believe that we can swoop in and save the day, no matter how bleak it looks. What happens when we keep our superhero myth alive?

- Our resources are spread too thin and nothing gets done well or on time.

- Things slip through the cracks and don't happen at all.

- People aren't clear on what's really important and make mistakes.

- Morale and engagement go down drastically.

- We ignore problems that start getting larger and larger.

- Decision-making takes longer.

- Employees burn out and need to be replaced, which costs more money.

Ultimately your business is impacted on multiple levels when the tough calls don't happen quickly. What steps can you take to make the right calls at the right times and simplify what you're doing?

B.   Pushing Back on Directives that Won't Possibly Work

Annie is a brand manager at a large packaged-goods company. Lately she's been asked to do more with less, and she's been falling behind. Instead of letting her manager know, she's been working long hours and pushing her team to make deadlines they can't possibly reach. Annie is at the end of her rope when her boss asks her how it's going, and she tells him she can't make a mission-critical deadline in the next week. Annie's mistake wasn't missing the deadline; it was not telling him when he could still do something about it!

When your management tells you to do the impossible, make sure they have a realistic view of what can and cannot be accomplished. When you communicate up front about what's do-able, it gives your leaders time to recalibrate. It also makes you more trustworthy in their eyes, particularly when you reset expectations and achieve what you say you can realistically do.

C.   Making Hard Decisions that Align with Organizational Strengths

Jeff Furst of Furst Person Inc. had a successful staffing agency for call centers. After five years on the job, he decided that what his clients needed was assessment software that would help them evaluate candidates more effectively. He abandoned the core business to focus on developing the software. Unfortunately, his clients weren't as excited about the idea and without the revenue from the temp business, they were cash-poor for a few years until landing their first large assessment engagement. His lesson: not to abandon a proven idea that drives your economic engine for an unproven one that might not.

When you have to make tough decisions, make them from strengths. What does your organization do best? What are your people excellent at?

D.   Finding the "Next Most Important Thing"

Use a simple "stop, start, continue" exercise to determine what you can stop altogether, what you need to start, and what must be continued. Get together the best and brightest on your team to assist in this prioritization exercise, and communicate the results clearly so that everyone understands their next most important actions.

Doing this on a regular basis can make work more productive, and can stop unnecessary wheel spinning!

TRY THIS
Stop... Start... Continue.

Convene your team for a meeting of at least two hours. An experienced facilitator can be helpful with this exercise.

1. On three separate flip charts, write the headings "Stop," "Start," and "Continue".

2. If the team is ten members or under, give each individual a pen and a stack of large notes.

3. Take fifteen minutes of silence to have everyone write down what they believe the team should stop, start, and continue.

4. If the team is bigger, create a series of small groups and give each group the stack of notes to use together. Take fifteen minutes for small group discussion on what should start, stop, and continue. Have a team captain write down the group's answers on the notes.

5. Take five minutes to have the participants put the notes in each area.

6. Take ten minutes to have the group cluster the responses.

7. Once the group has clustered the responses, take time as a large group to discuss the results and surface any conflict. The goal of the exercise is to make decisions that clearly enable to group to stop what needs to end, to start things that need to happen, and to continue what is working well.

E. Communicating—and Communicating the Same Message All Over Again

Here are three effective tips for communicating about changes in your organization or on your team. These tips apply for an increasingly virtual workplace.

1. Craft a simple message and restate it over and over again.

2. You can't communicate too much, particularly during a change that may make people uneasy or concerned. If you can marry transparency with empathy, it will go a long way. This message is something I have already repeated over ten times in this book, and I may do so again! See how you'll remember this one?

3. Get specific. What exactly does this mean for each stakeholder group? What exactly does the change you're experiencing mean behaviorally? By delivering clear, specific messages to the right people, you'll avoid major headaches. For example, if you're communicating about a layoff or downsizing, it's important not to focus on the details of the layoff itself, but to focus on what happens next. Who will be responsible for what? How will this enable the organization to improve in the face of challenging times? What do you expect from each person on your team that may look different?

4. Facilitate dialog. Let people ask questions, vent, and get used to the idea of things being different.

TRY THIS

Team Exercise: Building Team Community

We know that one of the top ways to keep a team functioning at its peak is to develop a shared sense of the possible future, to work toward it together, and to create a sense of loyalty and community that enables the group to be flexible when challenges come. We can develop our resilience through a sense of belonging.

Community enables employees to weather challenging times, and keeps them coming back to do so. It is community that allows us to belong to something greater than ourselves.

Building team community requires consistent, ongoing rituals. These can be as simple as the way a meeting is called to order, or as complex as a team-building exercise. Moods are the other important element that we forget when building team community. Positive effect is an indicator of team engagement, performance, and resilience. Laughter, even from something "corny," can have a positive impact on lightening the mood.

Instructions: Appreciating Team Strengths Exercise

Take a few minutes to write answers to the following questions:

1. At the end of each team meeting (this may be weekly or monthly), take ten minutes to conduct an appreciation exercise. The group facilitator or leader asks everyone to please offer at least one individual acknowledgment of someone on the team— it can be for something they've done or just for an attribute they bring to the table.

2. Introducing the exercise: "We're going to take ten minutes at the wrap of each meeting to institute a new team process. Each of us must be acknowledged for something he or she has contributed or is actively contributing to the group. It is an opportunity to say thank you and to be acknowledged. Anyone can start, but we will not end until each person has both given and received a comment."

3. Watch to make sure that each person has been thanked.

4. At the end, say a group 'thank you' and exit. Repeat at every team meeting.

Alignment Practice #2: Building Relationships and Community

I was meeting with the leadership team of a company in the Midwest to plan an initiative for the upcoming year. One of them said, "Are there really any organizations that have a true sense of community? Is any organization really engaged?"

Luckily, I have seen enough to be able to say YES!

Absolutely, there are many organizations that are successful in building relationships and community and the feeling is palpable. It starts at the level of teams. Teams rely on common goals, positive working relationships, and a sense of community.

When we look at a work team, having a shared identity is the difference between a standard working group and a functioning community. A workplace that is a fully functioning community is a place where people care about the work and each other. They feel a sense of pride and identity. They smile and say hello to each other and you can tell they enjoy coming to the office. They trust that someone has their back, and that the work will get done through collective effort, not just by individual superstars. As our social norms change, we are even more dependent on the workplace to meet our need for community and connection.

Sociologist Robert Putnam, author of Bowling Alone: The Collapse and Revival of the American Community, points out that over the last twenty-five years, attendance at club meetings has fallen 58 percent, family dinners are down 33 percent, and having friends visit is down 45 percent.

Healthy organizations understand that community is not something to take lightly, and when people have a sense of trust, relationship, and community at work, they are more likely to be productive, loyal, and engaged. The Gallup organization has pioneered research in the arena of high-performance work groups, and has found that one of the great predictors of team engagement and productivity is having a "best friend" at work. When people answer the question, "I have a best friend at work" in the affirmative, they are really saying they have relationships that transcend the transactional. They are saying there is someone they can trust.

Community comes from taking the time to know each other. It can be as simple as setting aside time to connect personally once per month, or you may want to invest in team-building sessions that build relationship and understanding, and help you get work done more smoothly.

Three things to remember when focusing on community as a team are:

- Orient the group to the values, mission, and/or purpose of the organization.

- Discuss the shared purpose of the team—why does this specific group exist?

- Define how the team fits within the larger structure—why is this group important to the rest of the organization?

Alignment Practice #3: Viewing Challenges as Opportunities

When Karen Goins was the Director of Purchasing Product Development at Navistar, a manufacturer of trucks, engines, and school buses, they needed to adapt to meeting new emissions standards, which required new parts and new technology, or they would no longer be able to sell their engines in the U.S.

In order to make Navistar's business viable within the next two years, they were launching twenty products at the same time and were responsible for purchasing twenty-eight million in materials per year.

Karen's team consisted of sixty-eight people working to place the products before production (buy materials, select suppliers, manage costs). Quality, tooling, buyers all reported to Karen, and they did not like each other.

When Karen was asked to take this job, it was a crisis situation. They needed the team to get it together, and fast.

Karen's first meeting with those who directly reported to her was supposed to be a status report. They turned their backs on each other and walked out of the room. "I almost ran into my old office and hid under my desk," she said. "I called it the Hatfields and the McCoys—they were people at war." It wasn't a team. It was just a diverse group of people with nothing in common. I had the challenge of rebuilding a team who feared they couldn't make it. The stakes were really high.

Karen's first step was to get to know the players. "I had to get out and talk to the people. They'd never had a director who walked around and talked to them. I had to gradually chip away at the walls that were up." The first challenge was looking at fairness and equality. There was a golf outing scheduled, and Karen's first response was to note that none of the women played, and the outing seemed exclusionary and antithetical to the kind of team spirit she needed to instill. She learned quickly that attempting to shut their fun down was going to go nowhere. "They wanted an excuse to not like me, so I had to pick my battles."

Karen had to keep repeating messages about the value of teamwork, working together, and sharing resources. They had never even talked about sharing resources—they were used to stealing people from each other when they could have all benefited by being a team focused on the bigger picture: the success of the whole. "They had never come together to talk about the whole—it was always the parts. There was no team - it was all 'me,' not 'we.'"

Karen also set out to prove the value of this organization to the larger company; the larger organization didn't value them or their input, and that had to change. Karen worked with the rest of the organization to promote the value of her formerly disenfranchised team. "These guys had low expectations. I had to raise those expectations and start giving them the belief that they were worthy. They did not want to change, but part of that was they couldn't see what was possible."

They had an expert mentality: If you don't know what I do, you're not important. They had to change that mentality completely. Karen took the stance that she was not there to learn everyone's jobs; she was there to help them be at their best and to perform. Gradually, they began to trust and understand that they were hired for their expertise, and they were responsible for that knowledge. They stopped being threatened by each other and started to view themselves as a team.

Karen also had to get rid of some people. Those were the people who tried to manipulate the team for their own benefit. They were not going to play nice. Everything was always wrong. They were complainers and blamers. "I needed truth tellers, and the backstabbers had to go. They bubbled to the top because I said it wasn't okay."

When the toughest, oldest, crabbiest, most change-averse guy began to change, that was quite a moment. He was a hardcore right-wing conservative working for Karen, a black woman. She said, "I was too far-out for him. He did what he wanted to do when he wanted to do it, and I thought he would never cut it but he began to care about his team". It was a true breakthrough and a milestone for Karen.

> I brought in fun. I got one of those books we all get in corporations. I bought a lot of them for fifty dollars [as well as] coins that said, 'I appreciate you' or 'Thanks.' I gave them to my direct reports, and told them to give them out for little things, whenever they do something nice. Give too many out versus too few. People had pride in the little knickknacks on their desks.

> Speaking up for your team, delivering on time, standing up and delivering a status report with everything up-to-date, being kind to someone, were things that people were ignoring. So I brought in acknowledgement. The little things in people's lives were acknowledged. Everyone had an acknowledgment on their birthdays. The things that matter to people aren't necessarily about the workplace, but this was about community. I wanted people to fight to get on my team rather than fight to get off.

The team had off-site meetings where they discussed everything from playing well together to being one voice to the rest of the company, and not coming out and saying, "I don't agree with it, but I'm going along with it".

That took time. They didn't want to come to the meetings and they would show up late. Karen stood her ground. They brought out the piggy bank; everyone who was late had to pay a dollar. Over time, there was less and less money in the jar.

They'd been under intense stress and pressure, but through the team's hard work, two years later, they delivered on every goal. The team was sad to see Karen go when she was pulled back to corporate after that fast success. "It was so rewarding to me to see what is possible with a team that seems broken. I never learned their jobs; my job was to lead them and help them to accomplish their goals, and I was able to do just that."

TRY THIS

Leading Your Team Through Crisis:
Building Alignment on Your Team

Facilitate a team discussion about Alignment. You may want an external facilitator for this one.

Step One: Convene the group for a two-hour session (or shorter depending upon your team's attention span and level of overwhelm). Let them know that the purpose of the session is to develop long-term strategies for releasing fear-based behavior, and operating from a higher level of resilience.

Step Two: Introduce the concept, and give each individual a chance to look at the team from the perspective of fear versus Alignment. Use the table below and ask people to rate themselves from zero to ten around each attribute of Alignment. For example, on the spectrum of shying away from action versus taking empowered action, are they a zero (shying away from action completely), a five (somewhere in the middle), or a ten (taking empowered action at all times)? Ask them to do the same snapshot assessment for their team that they did for themselves.

Step Three: Ask the group to discuss their responses. How do their individual scores impact their effectiveness? How do their team scores impact their effectiveness?

Step Four: How can you use the four practices as a team to maximize effectiveness, productivity, and Alignment?

FEAR	ALIGNMENT
Worry about what's next/what's coming	Confident that whatever happens you will make it through
0.........1............2............3............4............5............6............7............8............9............10	
Shying away from action	Taking empowered action
0.........1............2............3............4............5............6............7............8............9............10	
Feeling negative or pessimistic about the future	Feeling positive or optimistic about the future
0.........1............2............3............4............5............6............7............8............9............10	
Disconnecting from others	Reaching out to build relationships
0.........1............2............3............4............5............6............7............8............9............10	
Tolerating chaos	Practicing discipline
0.........1............2............3............4............5............6............7............8............9............10	
Focusing on survival issues	Focusing on self-esteem, self actualization, or transcende
0.........1............2............3............4............5............6............7............8............9............10	

Alignment Practice #4: Practicing Physical and Mental Discipline

When we think about practicing physical and mental discipline as a team, what does that mean? The first step is to make sure expectations are clear and that practices are outlined for everyone. I like to think about great sports teams and the expectations that a great coach sets for behavior and teamwork.

Starting with some simple ground rules that are outlined at the beginning of every meeting can re-enforce behavioral expectations. Here are some great examples of team ground rules:

1. **Assume best intentions.** Instead of judging, presume that all input is coming from an individual's best intentions for the good of the team. When we assume the best, we are less defensive, protective, agitated, and we become more open to dialog and input from diverse stakeholders.

2. **Straight talk.** Say what you have to say upfront, not after the fact or behind the back! When teams agree to say what they need to say upfront, there's less complaining, and gossip is not tolerated. If there are questions from the team, they are encouraged, not squelched.

3. **One team, one dream.** We offer each other help and ask for help to get the job done. We have each other's backs and think "we," versus just "me".

4. **Learn from mistakes.** We remove blame from any scenario and learn from problems, challenges, and mistakes. This gives permission and structure to talk about any blocks to success, or mistakes that have been made, without creating negative emotions, blaming, or punishing behaviors.

5. **Total responsibility.** We are all responsible for team goals being met. This means we watch out for each other and help solve any problems together that might block us from reaching goals. Instead of watching out just for ourselves, we have total responsibility for our team.

6. **Stay healthy.** We are focused on our own wellbeing and that of others.

Another set of action steps for team discipline? Create specific processes that are adhered to for conflict, for decision-making, and for taking breaks for fun together.

One of the toughest times to practice discipline is during team conflict. Conflicts can come from many places—personalities, values of team members at odds, limited resources, lack of clarity, or competition. There are conflicts that are constructive, that help us hear multiple points of view and highlight any blocks or challenges to success, and then there are conflicts that are destructive, the personal, energy-sapping, emotional conflicts of personality and of fear.

TRY THIS

Facilitating Team Conflict: A Simple Strategy

I have facilitated many teams, and I've found that there are few things more important than helping people be heard, and listening to others. Depending upon the level of conflict, you may want an outside facilitator for this exercise. Set up a specific time outside of your regular operational meetings to have a team meeting devoted to clearing the air and getting the team to be more productive.

1. State your shared objectives as a group.

2. Tell the group why it is important to address conflicts so that the team can benefit from diverse opinions or viewpoints rather than get stuck in them.

3. Begin a dialog about whatever challenges your team is facing. You will find that there are people who become emotional—frustrated, angry, challenging, or shutdown. Ask people to slow down. Use an object to represent a "talking stick" and have each person speak only when they are holding it. After someone has spoken, ask others to say what they just have just heard. This allows the person who just spoke to feel listened to. Repeat until each person on the team has had his or her say.

4. Decide how the group will come to a decision: Will the leader make the call, will there be a vote, or is there another process? Ask the group if they will align to whatever decision is made, even if it is not their first choice. Alignment allows the group to move forward as a cohesive unit. Make the decision.

5. Ask the group if they are aligned. Tell them the venting is done; we are now moving forward.

6. Give them behavioral guidelines to check in on at the next meeting. For example: listen to each other; respect that others have valuable opinions; if you are angry or defensive, step back and wait until you have cooled off.

Motivating and Engaging your Team:
Tapping into a Larger Purpose

"A pitcher cries for water to carry, a person for work that is real."

—Marge Piercy

Taking what we know about leading in crisis, we can take it one step further —beyond crisis and into the realm of transcending our norm, envisioning something new and greater.

At the World Economic Forum, world business leaders called for the urgent shift to a moral economic framework and in 2017 it set up "the Centre for the Fourth Industrial Revolution Network…to ensure that new and emerging technologies will help—not harm—humanity in the future". Headquartered in San Francisco, the network launched centers in China, India and Japan in 2018 and is rapidly establishing locally run Affiliate Centers in many countries around the world.

A report released in 2019, The State of Moral Leadership in Business by LRN, showed that "94% of managers who lead with moral authority and not just the authority that comes with their status, were seen as effective at achieving business goals".

Corporations and small companies have the capacity to tap into larger purpose in ways that cut costs, address needs through relevant products and services, and ultimately enhance the bottom line of the company. There is such a thing as profit AND people.

Profit AND planet. Profit AND joy, fulfillment, contribution, and employee satisfaction. And, and, and...

Every day I read new headlines about innovations that are enhancing the bottom line, reducing costs, and changing the world for the better. "Burger King to Power Restaurant with Energy Generated by Drive-Thru," "A New

Way to Turn Plastic into Fuel," "Abandoned Ford Motor Co. Plant to Become Renewable Energy Manufacturing Park," fill my inbox.

When we help our work-teams feel part of something larger, we are building momentum and positivity that builds performance, as well as relationships and community. It might be as simple as sharing with your team the amazing things your company is doing!

At P&G, their Children's Safe Drinking Water program has resulted in new hires who want to work for a company they can believe in.

Procter & Gamble's Safe Water

Procter & Gamble has a mission "to improve the lives of the world's consumers". When water was identified as one of the largest global problems, P&G began a partnership with the Center for Disease Control, focused on finding ways to provide clean water. Then they brought in a committed, experienced leader who was not afraid to fight for what he believed in—enter Greg Allgood, Ph.D.

> I was at a mud hole. It's the source of water for cattle, bathing, and drinking. I was there with CARE and U.S. AID. We asked a woman if we could treat her water with one of our P&G Purifier of Water packets. The packets work on water that is completely contaminated. This muddy, dirty water that most of us would not walk through for fear of disease was their only water supply. Through ripping open a small packet, stirring it into the water, and straining through some t-shirt fabric, and waiting, this cholera-infected, contaminated water became a pure source for drinking and bathing. The woman gave us her bucket of water to treat. She was so excited to see the clean, clear water. Then our conversation had us walk down to the edge of the water. A man snuck up and stole the woman's purified water—it was so valuable that it was taken as soon as we left it.

That was the moment Greg Allgood just knew this was a life-saving product that meets fundamental human needs.

The Children's Safe Water Project has provided one hundred and sixty million packets. Procter & Gamble doesn't make money on the packets themselves, but the VALUE to the company is far in excess of what they would make if they were attempting to make a profit on it. This is a great point of pride for Procter & Gamble's employees, and it demonstrates P&G's clear commitment to its mission. It's extremely visible. People join the company, citing the Children's Safe Drinking Water program as the reason they are doing so. With one hundred thousand employees, getting and retaining the best talent is a strategic priority for the organization.

Another value to the organization? Procter & Gamble is going into countries like Malawi, Ethiopia, Uganda—and they're saving lives, but that's not all. They're learning about the government and about distribution structure. Later, they will come in with other for-profit products that improve people's lives. Here's an example of the incredible power this gives the Procter brand in these markets. In Malawi, the minister of health introduced P&G and said, "I hear they are like [a competitive organization], but they are here to save lives, and we welcome them into our country and hope they bring more of their products".

Dr. Allgood tells another story of the power of this program to forward the P&G brand:

> Bob McDonald was in Columbia meeting with President Arribe
> to discuss the importance of Procter & Gamble's Latin America
> expansion. Two weeks later, there were big floods in Toluma,
> Colombia, that affected thousands of Columbian people,
> including their water security. The president himself called and
> asked for Water Purifier packets, asking if he could fly his private
> plane to pick the packets up. Employees in Latin America said it
> was the highlight of their careers distributing those packets to

people in need. The president of Columbia was on the news saying how great P&G was. You could never pay for that.

While mission statements and shared values set the tone for purposeful action, you can also opt to give your team the experience of doing something purposeful together.

Volunteering together can build relationships and community, can give participants a greater sense of meaning and purpose, and can build those elusive positive emotions when a team is stressed out. It takes people out of their day-to-day environment and helps them see their colleagues in a new way.

TRY THIS

Team-Building by Community-Building

Volunteering together can be a simple way to share a group experience, do something positive for a not-for-profit organization, and serve your greater community.

Through that shared experience, teams have time to get to know each other better, to create something of value quickly, and to build positive emotions. This kind of experience can be a few hours, a day, or if you're REALLY in the mood for a workout, you can take your show on the road for a weeklong program abroad through one of many organizations that do "volunteer tourism".

Initial Steps for the Team Leader to Take:

- Either alone or with a small task force, make the decision which organization or project your team will take on.

- Approve the session with HR and find out if you have a matching grants/gifts program.

- Make sure there are roles for everyone, including those with specific disabilities, if applicable.

- Arrange for a pre-meeting in which you prepare the team, and then arrange for the actual volunteering. Make sure you hand out instructions on paper with directions, logistics, contact information, and a paragraph about the organization or project.

To Discuss with the Team in Preparation for a Day of Volunteering:

Why are we volunteering together? What are your goals? They may be building team cohesion, taking time away from the office for a reset, integrating new team members, or understanding a specific audience to whom your company provides products or services.

During the Project:

Make sure your team is fed and watered appropriately, and that they take breaks if it is a physically strenuous task.

After the Project:

Arrange for a debrief meeting to discuss how the day went and to focus on the gains for the team. In that session, ask the following positive questions:

1. What is one thing you learned about someone on our team that you didn't know before?

2. How did getting out of the office and focusing on something else help our team?

3. What worked well?

4. What can we feel good about after our shared experience?

When we have a strong team ethic, clear roles and responsibilities, positive relationships, good communication, and a clear understanding of what we're working toward together, our teams are set up for success.

Why then do we see teams fail after doing so much work to make them strong?

Teams are made up of individuals, of course, and individuals have clear gains when they operate from fear. If you're hitting a wall and still see fear-based behavior rearing its head, it's time to look at why fear takes hold and stays there. What do we have to lose by changing for the better? Take a look at the next chapter to find out.

Chapter 8
What We Gain Individually
from Living in Fear

"People have a hard time letting go of their suffering. Out of their fear of the unknown, they prefer suffering that is familiar."

—Thich Nhat Hanh

First, we have to acknowledge the real—and look at how fear works. Since it's fear that stops us, how can we understand it and address the reality of our human response to the unknown, to stress, and to change?

Gain #1: Self-Protection

How are you protecting yourself in ways that don't serve you? What self-protection do you need to give up? Are there risks you haven't taken because of your fear of loss, failure, or change?

TRY THIS

Identifying Opportunities to Challenge Yourself

My colleague, Deborah Shea, calls this the "walking through fire" exercise.

Take a piece of paper and draw three boxes, one inside of the other.

In the central square, write "SAFE." Think about the areas in which you play it safe. Write them in the center. By writing out what you do that keeps you safe, you can learn where you might want to push further.

In the next level, write "CALCULATED RISK".

Think of the areas in which you could stretch to take a calculated risk. Write that down in the calculated risk box. In this area, these are healthy challenges you're taking on.

On the outside level, write "WALK THROUGH FIRE".

In this final level, write down what you would do if you knew that you could walk through fire and not get burned. What are the big risks to you that you are not taking? Why not? What fears are stopping you? Are they realistic?

Use this exercise to start pushing yourself into greater levels of challenge and growth.

Gain #2: The Rewards of Victimhood

"One of the fundamental differences between the Victim Orientation and this one [Creator] is where you put your focus of attention...For Victims, the focus is always on what they don't want: the problems that seem constantly to multiply in their lives... Creators, on the other hand, place their focus on what they do want."

—David Emerald

Many of us have been victims of events beyond our control. It may have been a small thing (The bus didn't come; I am doomed to a life of lateness) or a considerably more terrible thing (I was hit by the bus and lost my ability to walk). With both big and small events, we need a chance to process our feelings. For some, it will take longer than others, but if we stay too long in the victim perspective, there are a number of things it does for us that keep us wanting more.

1. Victims get help and sympathy, and deserve to be cared for.

2. Victims are justified in feeling angry, helpless, and hopeless, and get to be "right" about their reality.

3. Victims do not have to take responsibility for their role in their victimization. It's someone else's fault.

There is an important step when one has been victimized to grieve, get help, to feel one's feelings, to declare that we are not to blame, and to remember we are worthy of goodness.

Victims have a right to get help, sympathy and care. They have a right to feelings of anger, hopelessness, and helplessness. But there may be a point where it moves into victimhood.

In organizations, we have patterns of victimhood or patterns of empowerment. I worked in one organization where the tendency toward victimhood was so big that water-cooler conversations often turned into competitions for who had it the worst. "I had to stay here until three in the morning," says one. "You think that's bad? I had to give up all of my vacations last year," says the next. "You think that's bad? I missed my kid's baseball season and he's not talking to me now." And it goes on from there. One thing to know about victimhood—it's catching!

Sometimes when we talk about our power, we are rejected by those who wish we would stay in a state of victimhood so they can take care of us, relate to us, or even keep us less powerful in order to feel superior.

To get rid of victimhood, we need to shift our sense of powerlessness to one of empowerment. If we go back to the attributes of resilience, we need to tap our positivity, proactivity, and reframing in order to get out of a victim stance and into one of action.

In a recent workshop I facilitated on resilience, I spoke with a man who had experienced a terrible automobile accident in which two of his family members had died. For this man, there was no way he could ever believe that there was meaning in his experience, and he would never feel like he was a survivor; he would always be a victim. If he started moving on with his life from a place of strength, he believed he would be saying that the events didn't matter, didn't hurt him. He felt he was protecting the memory of his family, and ultimately he was protecting himself from hoping again and repeating his devastating loss.

We don't just protect ourselves from negative emotions and experiences; we also protect ourselves from the risk of experiencing positive emotions because of our vulnerability.

Researcher, George Vaillant, documented in a longitudinal study of men in Massachusetts, those who bounced back from change and challenge. Joshua Shenk commented in *The Atlantic*, on Vaillant's lecture to a group of positive psychology students:

> Vaillant said that positive emotions make us more vulnerable than negative ones. One reason is that they're future-oriented. Fear and sadness have immediate payoffs—protecting us from attack or attracting resources at times of distress. Gratitude and

joy, over time, will yield better health and deeper connections—but in the short term actually put us at risk. That's because, while negative emotions tend to be insulating, positive emotions expose us to the common elements of rejection and heartbreak.

To illustrate his point, he told a story about one of his "prize" Grant Study men, a doctor and well-loved husband. "On his seventieth birthday," Vaillant said, "when he retired from the faculty of medicine, his wife got hold of his patient list and secretly wrote to many of his longest-running patients, 'Would you write a letter of appreciation?' And back came one hundred single-spaced, desperately loving letters—often with pictures attached. She put them in a lovely presentation box covered with Thai silk, and gave it to him". Eight years later, Vaillant interviewed the man, who proudly pulled the box down from his shelf. "George, I don't know what you're going to make of this," the man said, as he began to cry, "but I've never read it". "It's very hard," Vaillant said, "for most of us to tolerate being loved".[22]

[22] Joshua Wolf Shenk, "What Makes Us Happy" *The Atlantic,* June 2009

TRY THIS

Stuck Thinking to Power Thinking

Write down a list of anything that you are unhappy with in your work. It could be a new strategy, a colleague you have trouble working with, a policy you don't like, the hours you keep, anything at all.

To move out of the disempowered perspective, for each one of these items, think about your choices—are you willing to accept this reality and move on, or do you need to take action?

The final column is for any next steps. You've made the choice…now what are you going to do?

SCENARIO	CHOICE (ACCEPTANCE OR ACTION)	NEXT STEP

Gain #3: Staying Connected to the Past

Washington, D.C. psychiatrist Steven Wolin, M.D., and Sybil Wolin, Ph.D., are researchers and practitioners in the arena of resilience, and they offer survivors of troubled families a more balanced perspective about their past, based on twenty years of research on adult children of alcoholics.

Most survivors do not repeat their parents' drinking patterns. The same is true of adults who have survived families troubled by mental illness, chronic marital disputes, racial discrimination, and poverty.

Most people mistakenly operate on what Steven Wolin calls "the damage model," a false belief about the way disease is transmitted. The belief is that if your family has problems, you will inherit them. One of the reasons we stick to the damage model is that it gives us a connection—albeit a not-so-nice connection—to our family, to the people who raised us or gave us our genetic material. But this way of thinking must be turned around because the vast majority of us have some challenge in our family of origin or childhood, and the vast majority of us don't inherit what we choose to reject from our backgrounds.

Arden, a tall, blond sales executive with a track record of bringing in enormous numbers for her organization, entered executive coaching with a belief that she was damaged, and that no matter what success she had, failure was just around the corner. As the adult child of two alcoholic parents, Arden took on the belief that if she was not always vigilant, disaster would strike. She had been passed over for promotion twice, specifically because of her level of stress and its impact on those she managed. Ultimately, she believed that her level of stress and hyper-vigilance was protecting her from sudden devastation.

As she began to look carefully at this set of beliefs, she told me that her most important insight was that the stress she was experiencing was sabotaging her, not protecting her, and that she was ready to start focusing on her successes, rather than worrying about "what if".

In order to put a stop to her belief in her own damage, Arden had to take an inventory of the attributes that existed in her parents, and look at what she did and did not inherit. After a realistic assessment, she was faced with the truth—she had inherited physical features, intellectual curiosity, the desire for order and organization, but she had not inherited alcoholism or violence. When Arden acknowledged the real, she found that instead of the truth scaring her and stopping her, the truth did indeed set her free.

"Is it as easy as all that?" you may ask. The answer is yes. When we transform our beliefs, it happens in an instant, and there's no going back. When we move from believing that we are damaged to knowing that we can

154

choose our own path, that transformation is permanent. We may experience momentary doubts, old messages or thoughts, but they are only ghosts.

Gain #4: Not Having to Be Conscious

Many of us are caught in a spiral of unconscious "self-talk" that underlies our conscious activity. We have an undercurrent of negative "self-hypnosis" that continuously tells us what our unconscious believes to be true. If we ignore it, not only do we get to hang on to the status quo, we really don't have to challenge ourselves to think differently. That "self-talk" can come from old messages that were given to us by our parents, on the playground, anywhere.

I had the opportunity to interview Wendi Freisen, who is one of the most successful hypnosis experts in the world and the most searched hypnotist on the web. She has worked with CEOs, pro-athletes, and thousands of others to stop the spiral of negative self-hypnosis and change the way we think. Here's part of our interview:

> Wendi Freisen: We spend so much effort trying to make something change. We use will power. We make commitments. We go on a new diet. We exercise. We decide we're never going to get angry again. We're going to be patient. But it is *futile*. The conscious mind is so powerless compared to what's happening in that other-than-conscious area, that thing that we can't really explain, that's reactive, and it's being triggered below our awareness, and things are happening before we have a chance to apply will power. Does that make sense?
>
> You're there working and you know you've got to make some really big accomplishments to keep your job, but you don't know why you're out of energy. You're feeling hopeless. You don't have any creativity and you don't have any drive. Consciously, you're saying, "Today, I'm going to go in there and make such a difference. I'm going to crush it at the board meeting". But

you're operating from a core belief of fear and hopelessness - I'm so stressed out. I'm tired all the time. The economy is in the dumps.

At the same time, your conscious mind is trying to get you up for the game. So now you've created an additional problem, which is the conflict between that will power and drive that you're trying to create in your conscious mind and the underlying belief that it's not going to work. So, you have this battle that's going on inside of you constantly.

We're not even fully present about the fact that we do have negative statements that we're saying that have a tremendous amount of power. So if you find yourself engaging in conversation with others that is about the negative state of our economy, the negative state of your health or you say to someone, "Oh, you know, my insomnia is so bad, I just can't sleep at night because I'm so worried about everything and I wake up in the morning just a bundle of nerves," well, what you're doing is reinforcing that very thing that you supposedly don't want.

Candice Pert showed how our molecules of emotion in our brain light up more memories and look for more similar emotions. It floods your body with chemicals that put you in that exact state that you're trying to overcome. We need to learn positive self-hypnosis. We need to change those molecules of emotion, and start flooding our bodies with immune-building, positive chemicals. We end up healthier, physically and mentally.[23]

So what do we need to do to get over the block of negative self-hypnosis? Find a new message to replace the negative!

---

[23] Interview with Wendi Freisen, Voice America Radio, World Changers Radio with Karlin Sloan, 2009

Exercise to Replace Negative Thoughts

Learning to reframe our reality is a critical part of our relationship to the external environment. If we can control our thoughts we can impact our physiology and our behavior, and what happens around us. Negative thoughts tend to extend out into the future, so watch how you impact what happens by envisioning the negative.

STIMULUS / OBJECTIVE REALITY	NEGATIVE THOUGHT	REPLACEMENT THOUGHT
Example: If the payments aren't made next month, our house will be foreclosed upon	**Example:** We're going to lose our house, and this is just the start of things spiralling out of control. Our family is in danger of splitting apart because of the instability and stress.	**Example:** We might lose our house, but through this we'll learn to communicate as a family, and we'll teach our children that money isn't everything.

Gain #5: Hanging On to Guilt Rather than Taking Action

In order to move into a state of Alignment, we need to let go of what bogs us down. Sometimes that block is guilt that emerges from our past, when we have done things that we feel ashamed of, and we continue to focus on that bad action. It may be the fear of repeating past bad actions, or fear of the terrible consequences that arise when we do things that are wrong for ourselves and others. Whether you are a leader, a manager, or a contributor to an organization, your ability to forgive yourself is critical to your ability to deal effectively with change. If we hang on to guilt, we can't move forward.

A leader in helping people see beyond fear and suffering, Thich Nhat Hanh is a venerable Buddhist monk from Vietnam. His life and work have been dedicated to the cessation of suffering and to bringing about peace. He has been a leader in the Engaged Buddhism movement, promoting the individual's active role in creating change.

Tich Nhat Hanh has worked equally with Vietnamese and American soldiers to remove their suffering and this has been controversial for some. His approach to life is the realization that all beings are interconnected. He calls this "inter-being". When we step away from our fear of the other and begin to look at what bonds us together, we create a shift. We are capable of listening, of understanding, and of empathy. Thich Nhat Hanh's life experience includes witnessing and escaping horrific violence. He encourages us to let go of the past and move into the future anew:

> 'If we stick to our suffering we can never stand up for healing and prepare the future for our children and their children. I would say to the Vietnam War veteran, 'Okay, you did kill five children. We know that. But you are here, alive, in the present moment. Do you know that you have the power to save five children today? You don't have to go to Vietnam or Southeast Asia. There are American children who are dying every day; they may need only one pill to be saved from their illness'.

Guilt points a large red arrow at whatever you need to work out in your life, whether it's a relationship that's gone awry, or knowledge of what's right that you didn't follow. Forgiveness is not always something focused on others; sometimes it's something you need for yourself. Before you can truly live with a clear conscience, take time to evaluate and learn from your mistakes.

TRY THIS

Forgiving Your Wrongdoings: A Journal Exercise

Activating compassion for yourself is easiest when you can remember that all of us make mistakes. Forgiveness is necessary when you can be specific about a deed that hurt others or yourself. Take your time in this journal exercise to explore what you've done in your life that you regret.

Make a list of those things that you regret. You may have lashed out at your child, spread a rumor that got someone fired, or relapsed with an addiction. You may have been complicit or participated in unethical actions in your organization, or you may have blown the whistle on someone and have gotten them in trouble. Think about what amends you have to make—are they direct apologies to someone, or is it better for you to just write down that you are sorry, or speak it to someone you trust?

Once you have your list, imagine you were counseling someone else who was coming to you for forgiveness. With your deepest compassion, write down what you would say to that person.

How do you know when you're complete? The memory of the mistake is there, but the sting is less. It is no longer part of your identity; it's an action you did in the past not to be repeated. You have learned what you will not do again.

The last step of forgiving yourself? Commitment to a new start and to following your conscience from now on. Forgiveness is a transformation, and the discomfort of this exercise is replaced by relief and clarity. Remember that it takes time, and that your relief will be equal to your compassion.

Gain #6: Hanging On To What We Know

When we cannot imagine the possibility of something better, why would we leave what we have? The fear of the unknown stops us from changing our circumstances.

Keith was the chief operating officer of an engineering firm, and had ongoing challenges with his boss, the owner and president. He was brought in to take the organization to the next level and quickly found out that wasn't what the founder wanted. From Keith's second month of work, he knew his boss didn't want to change and grow the organization. He spent three or four months trying to move the needle. He was doing the best he could to retain and develop star performers in what he termed "an abusive environment".

But he was only marginally successful, and not happy.

A long list of messages kept him in that job. "First, I thought I needed to be responsible to my family–I was going to be a father for the third time–and keep this job because I needed the income. I thought I might not find anything else. That was a valid idea, but it was an excuse. There were other options open to me and I knew it. At a certain point I realized I was absorbing more than my share of abuse."

"When Henry was born, I had this clarity about what was important. I saw that I'd be a miserable father if I continued to be miserable in my work. So, I quit three days after Henry's birth. I just knew it would be okay, and it was. I found the right job—it took a little time, but it was just right."

Is there something you hang on to that isn't serving you anymore? Is it familiar and comfortable? It's an easier route to stick with what we know, but it may stop us from taking a risk and discovering that change can be positive.

This concept holds for us as individuals and, in particular, in leadership. You see a way the organization could change for the better but you don't want to make waves. It's easier to just go along with what's happening now, even with

160

things you know aren't working. The worst-case scenario? We see what's not working and, instead of advocating for change, we complain and don't take action.

TRY THIS

Identifying What Could Be Changed for the Better

Before we can commit to a course of action and change what's not working, we have to be clear about the specifics of our situation. This exercise can be used in three scenarios: personal, team, and organization.

Often, when we look at our lives, we think of positives and negatives. In this exercise we take the attitude that either it's positive or it can be changed to be positive.

If we remember the victim thinking exercise, this one helps us to make choices as well. What do we want to keep? To accept? To change?

SAMPLE: My Team

Fill in the table below. Try to stay in balance with an equal amount in the left and right columns.

WHAT'S WORKING	WHAT COULD BE CHANGED FOR THE BETTER
I have almost all of the positions filled on my team.	I don't have the budget for a new hire and I am missing one person. I need to either advocate for it, or help get that role covered better than it is now.

161

Gain #7: Being Liked

We waste thousands of hours worrying about being liked, respected, or viewed in the positive.

In an interview with an anonymous sales executive, I heard about their process of letting go of the need to be liked:

> My pretense was that I've got pressure to produce results by building the quality and number of relationships I have in business. The problem was that I had started to see my world as a popularity contest that I think I can't win. Maybe I have always seen life that way since primary school. I would choose to not make sales calls because people might not like me. I was stopping myself because of being liked or not being liked.
>
> Then I had a huge breakthrough—I realized I don't have to do things just to work on being liked. You can say here's this guy, I don't like him, but I should get him to work with me. Like is irrelevant. "That guy doesn't like me" becomes irrelevant. If you have a compelling enough business proposition, it doesn't matter if people like you. It's really about the strength of what I was offering— and once I realized that, my sales efforts completely shifted. Now I'm making them an offer they can't refuse because it's no longer about me.

If you've ever been gripped by the desire for approval—from your family, your boss, your peers—then underneath that desire is some feeling of inadequacy or fear. When we want the approval of others, we are hoping for an external source to tell us that it's all going to be alright. Letting go of that need means learning to give approval to yourself.

Gain #8: Staying in Control

"Neurosis is the inability to tolerate ambiguity."

—Sigmund Freud

The first thing to remember about being in control is that we aren't! We may think we can control what happens in our lives, but really, we are not always

163

able to make reality exactly as we would like it. We are, however, able to have control specifically over our own actions and reactions to what is.

Dorie Ellzey Blesoff is a consultant in organizational learning and change, and an adjunct faculty member at Northwestern University at the School of Education and Social Policy. She has deep expertise in helping organizations deal with change and transition. She described to me the bittersweet nature of parenting during a time of transition, and the parallels of letting go as a parent to letting go at work:

> As parents, we wanted to help our daughter be a strong, empowered girl. My preschooler came home and said; "Brian's daddy said I can't be a doctor because I'm a girl, so I need to do something else when I grow up". She watched Wonder Woman! We were raising her to feel fearless and that she can do anything. One comment from a schoolmate's father and she was changing her career choice. But I couldn't control it. It's very complicated. You want to control the world for your kids, but your kids may make different choices than you want them to. They might have experiences you'd never wish for them.

We can try as hard as we can to control everything about our children's lives, but ultimately, we learn that they are separate from us, and that we can influence but can't control them or the environment around them. The alternative to staying in control is appreciating that the world is influenced and co-created by us, not controlled.

Dorie is a mother of three, and recently sent her youngest daughter off to college. After saying goodbye to her third child after thirty years of kids in the home, Dorie's question was, "Who am I if I am not daily mothering? Who am I if I'm not monitoring my kids homework and making sure they're fed and clothed and housed?" Dorie continued, "I've worked all through all three children; I have an identity as someone involved in work, very meaningful work. That isn't changing, but this year was challenging because

Marc retired; he's got a new path. Our kids have moved on but our son has come home temporarily; it's truly unknown how it will all play out".

The hardest thing of all about transition is about losing what you've identified as your identity. When we lose a job or change our career path, there's a time in which we don't know who we are anymore! The core may not have changed at all, but we haven't figured out how to express that core in a new way, in a new identity. What ends? What ends is who you used to be and how you used to behave.

Author William Bridges identified times of ambiguity and transition as "the neutral zone" between endings and new beginnings. When we are in the neutral zone, it's very creative. For Dorie:

> It's been so valuable for me and the leaders I've worked with. The neutral zone lasts a long time, and the hardest part is that you may feel very competent in a certain setting that you're used to. I've been mothering a long time. I'm competent at that. Now I'm stepping into a new realm, and what am I doing? You end up feeling incompetent for a period of time. There's something about the neutral zone that gives you time to process endings, and discover who you are that has not changed. You can now emerge and become something new.

In our modern business cultures, "ambiguity" is a bad word. People want a plan to execute. But ambiguity can be a great thing—a creative zone in which we undo what's not working and experiment.

When we take this into a work environment, we step into that neutral zone whenever we have an organizational change. It's a time when we can create what's next. It's a time to be proactive and to influence your future. If you have that attitude or orientation, it's time to build something new. It's exciting, if daunting!

In butterfly terms, there's a chrysalis and cocoon time when one type of being becomes another. The caterpillar needs that time to incubate before its butterfly wings can unfurl and fly.

When we're going through the neutral zone, particularly in organizations, we get frustrated. We don't know what to do. We don't feel competent. The strategy and vision aren't set. We haven't got the clarity that we want in order to move forward.

When you've done really well and your boss leaves, you may have an interim boss. It's not clear what the rules are, what their leadership style will be, what their expectations are. You could spend that whole time being sad or fearful or angry, but empowered people will be thinking about what they can do to positively impact the transition. Another example of finding yourself in the neutral zone is being acquired by another company, when you've felt loyal and proud of the old company. Your company name has changed, headquarters has changed, the identity of the organization has changed, and you don't know the rules yet.

It's a time that would be easy to spend being upset about the loss of control and knowing. During this time of ambiguity, instead of lapsing into 'normal' fear-based behaviors, there's an opportunity to learn about change, to figure out where you belong, what you do know, what you can offer, what actions you can take to make something positive out of the situation. It's a time to ask, "What is my vision for the future in the new organization? What can I do to make something positive out of this situation?"

Using times of ambiguity to create, to think, to reflect, and to lay the groundwork for the future is our great opportunity, versus attempting to stay in control of what's happening.

TRY THIS
Bridging Ambiguity

"On the road from the City of Skepticism, I had to pass through the Valley of Ambiguity." —Adam Smith

Take a moment to identify any ambiguity in your life. The opportunity for us in a state of transition is one of great creativity and opportunity. You can use times of ambiguity and not-knowing to tap all of your resilience attributes, to get proactive and envision the future you want. This can be an individual or group exercise, but if employed for a group this process needs an experienced facilitator. This dramatized exercise has a profound effect since it gets us out of the logical, linear mind and helps us to physically experience a new perspective.

Examples:

My company has been in flux and I don't know who my boss will be. My whole team is waiting for new direction.

Step One: Physically create a space with the past on one side, the future on the other, and a bridge in the middle. This can be outside or inside, and can be as literal or metaphoric as you want. It just needs to exist in physical space so that you can experience walking through transition and ambiguity.

Step Two: Write down phrases about your past, your role in the past, your identity in the past. Spend time with each item and think about what you need to leave behind you, and what you can take away with you. Write down what you'd like to take with you, and leave what you wrote about the past in that physical space.

Step Three: Walk across the bridge with what you're taking with you. As you walk across the bridge, you can set an intention about what can come next. Don't just wish for something; intend it, envision it, create a full image of what you want to influence or create for the future. Take time to enjoy the bridge, and stay there and think. What have you just let go? What creative opportunities do you have right now as you're walking into the future?

Step Four: Walk to the other side, and give thanks for what you've learned, what you're letting go of, and for the opportunity to move into a new future, no matter how unknown that future may be.

If it's a job you're letting go of, what are you getting rid of, leaving behind? What learning are you taking with you? What relationships do you want to maintain in the future?

This exercise is a physical, visceral way to experience transition and to really look at what you want to take with you from the past into the future.

Gain #9 – Staying in Power

Many of us that live in privileged positions benefit from a global system that is inherently built on inequality, injustice, and un-sustainability. We don't have an alternative, so we participate in the system as it is.

No one of us can change the system in which we operate alone, so we may try to band together with like-minded people to do what we believe is possible and to change our corner of the world for the better, but without audacious, massive change we are still benefitting from that same system.

Consciously or unconsciously, it's difficult for those who benefit from a system to want to change it.

Fear of losing power, status, privilege and benefits provided is a very powerful deterrent to creating new paradigms that will benefit our species many generations from now.

The Opportunity

The opportunity for unblocking our fear and defensiveness is the gift of approaching life from a perspective of openness, from collaboration, and from creativity. For all of these gains, the losses from operating from fear are far greater. So how do we get ourselves in the habit of Alignment?

Chapter 9

Personal Stories of the
Four Alignment Practices in Action

"The key to change...is to let go of fear."

—Rosanne Cash

So how do we start our own individual engines and stay inspired and inspiring? Why, the four practices of Alignment, of course!

- Accepting what is, and focusing on the future

- Building relationships and community

- Viewing challenges as opportunities

- Practicing physical and mental discipline

This chapter looks at how individual leaders have used the four practices to bounce back from adversity, and adapt to rapid change. These are all real people, real challenges, and real examples of the four alignment practices in action. These people have all seen crazy, unpredictable change in life and work, and lived to tell the tale.

The "C" Word

This story comes from Colleen Boselli, executive, mom, wife, coach and consultant, and cancer survivor.

Colleen Boselli had three children (six, seven, and a four-month-old baby) and was working full-time at an advertising agency in Boston as the director of account management, with over one hundred and twenty-five people in her department. But her husband had accepted a job offer in London and she'd recently resigned; she was hoping to take a little time off work to sort out new schools for her children.

Colleen did a self-breast examination and found a hard lump. "I got shaky and called the doctor. I was at work that morning and I couldn't concentrate on anything; it just didn't feel right. I saw the OBGYN, and they sent me immediately in a taxi over to the breast surgeon's office."

> I had a brand new baby, I was in good health, I was moving in six weeks... how could this be happening to me? The surgeon, a very grandfatherly man, in a dark, old, academic-looking office, said he was ninety-nine percent sure it was breast cancer. I needed to have surgery right away. You need to decide about reconstruction right away—it will only interfere with the process —all in ONE HOUR. My husband picked up the kids from school and daycare, and I went downstairs and went outside to walk to the train station. It was a familiar neighborhood but I just didn't know where I was. I'm a very practical person; it didn't take too long to get it together, so I found the train station. I went to the babysitters to pick up Jack, my young son, and cried to them about what happened. I had a flurry of meetings over the next couple of days. I found a new surgeon and went through the process with a woman who was a mom with whom I felt very comfortable. I took time to think and look at reality.

Colleen had the surgery on the first of July. She rescinded her resignation and took medical leave. "We undid the moving plan. My husband worked with an investment firm, and they got us out of all the commitments we had. Arnold [Colleen's employer] was phenomenal, how they took care of me. That community, those relationships—it was invaluable. They would call me and say, 'We will get you through this'. I have repeated that to people I've helped through cancer since. It was the most important thing they could have said. They were there with me".

Her husband went to every single treatment with her that she'd let him come to. He gathered information and acted as a second set of eyes. Another benefit of having a work community that cared.

Arnold even hired a gardening company that planted flowers around my house, watered them, and took care of them. They made my environment so beautiful. I took nine months off. I went from the surgery into chemo and radiation. I didn't let myself get sick. I was determined that I would be the poster-child of survivorship. It was stage-three cancer. I had the maximum dose of radiation. I felt tired, but I was determined not to be sick.

Colleen was going to make it in a way in which she could help other people:

I had no choice—I had three children, and I had to survive. I had a very positive mental attitude, and I did what I don't do anymore: I got lots of sleep, I joined a gym and took kickboxing when I was up for it. I had a little beanie cap on, and I was convinced I would be healthy. They helped me find a nanny who came to the house and took care of the baby and made sure I could get the sleep I needed through the process.

Colleen's husband still had an international role. He had a trip to Rome as the treatment process was ending, and she wanted to go with him. "Against the recommendations of everyone, I went straight from my last treatment after thirty-eight days of radiation to Logan Airport and flew right to Rome. A couple of weeks later I went back to work. I needed to get back to my old life." She would not be stopped! Her physical and mental discipline allowed her to stay focused, healthy, and careful:

After a couple of months, I switched to a part-time role. I had plenty of time to think about what I needed to do to stay healthy. I needed a much less stressful position. I believe that part of the reason I had the cancer is because of how stressed I was, and I thought about that. I thought about what were my greatest skills and talents, and how I would focus on those strengths, rather than just what I was capable of doing. I wanted to solve a need within Arnold, and we had just completed our first employee survey. Among the results we learned that the employee population was not crying for more money; they wanted more career development, leadership training, feedback. I worked with the chairman on the plan; I proposed a new department for talent development, and I ran that department, focusing on the top priorities.

In remaking her career, she found something she was passionate about, and helped the agency to thrive. When I spoke with Colleen, she talked about her illness as a gift:

Something so ironic about this…my husband one day was approached out of the blue about moving to London just last year, and here I am living in London with my husband and my four kids—they're older, but it's just perfect. I believe it was meant to be! I feel so privileged to have had breast cancer. I have helped other people become more resilient and get through things like this. I feel like now I can relate to anyone who is going through challenges; I can see the hope. They were skills that I had, but they weren't as tested and as polished as they became as a result of this experience. My perspective is that much more gelled and stronger because now I know how to help people see that situations may seem bleak, but with hope, a strategy, taking care of yourself, you can find a way through it. I think resilience comes directly from knowing your strengths and focusing on them. If you focus on what you have and what you can do, it will help through any challenge.

Three Strikes

Steve D'Amico was a Design Director at a global Fortune 100 company and Senior Faculty at the Centre for Creative Leadership at the Cincinnati University.

I had a wake-up year in 2001. I had to dig deep and think about things. My company was offering packages and downsizing and I was pissed off at them. It took me a while to figure out what was going on. It was like three strikes.

Strike one: Steve finds an old roll of film

> I got a new computer and computer bag and while I was cleaning out the old one I found a roll of black-and-white film which had been in there for years. I had the film developed—it was of my daughters at Hilton Head—their first experience of the beach. I realized I didn't remember it. Somehow, I was losing track. This was really important to me. It hit me hard. I was so angry at the company for taking all of my time. I wondered what I'd missed. I vented in what I now know is the wrong place.

Steve was blaming the company. He was convinced he needed to get out of his job if it was the last thing he did:

> I accepted a package. The deal was you had to look at your work and negotiate with your manager, looking at how long it would take to finish up and go. I accepted the package in July of '01. I said it would be April or May of '02. I felt lucky—they were paying me to leave. I thought the man was bringing me down and I had to get out.

Strike two—September 11.

> A colleague flagged me down, and my wife was trying to get a hold of me. My brother, Rob, had an office in the Twin Towers. I called my parents. I asked where my brother's office was. They said it was the Trade Center. I asked them to find anything they could with his mailing address. They couldn't find anything. I had to tell them that one of the towers had been hit. We couldn't verify where my brother was. No calls were going in and out of New York. I saw the second plane hit. We didn't find out until the next day; it turned out he had moved his offices five blocks

away. I watched the whole thing not knowing. For many of us, that was a day of "remember where you were." I'll always remember that. I was crying and feeling helpless. I was in shock for a while. So that was strike two. I didn't know what to do with it, except to say to myself, "Life is short".

Strike three:

Around Thanksgiving, my wife's eyesight started shutting down. She was having terrible headaches. The week before Christmas, after a number of MRI's, we went in to see the neurologist. He showed us there were spots on her brain. We knew what that was because Pam's sister had MS. As you might imagine, it was a pretty sober Christmas holiday. We knew a lot about MS, because Pam's sister was not very functional and we were scared. Some time in January, I woke up.

I looked at myself in the mirror with all the whining I'd been doing about my job. No man had been putting me down; it was me. There is no man. I'm the man. I knew in that moment what I had to do. We had to move back to Colorado where Pam's parents are. I said, "Now I know what's important".

Steve changed. He prioritized doing things his way.

People really noticed I was different. I was grateful. I was happy at work. I thought, "Life is short, I need to go to Colorado. I'll take a package and I'll figure it out". I told my boss. I talked to a colleague who had been working remotely from Dallas. I said no, I didn't want to work that way. A few people mentioned it to me, and I thought, "What the heck?" My boss and I didn't know if it would work, but we tried it. It did work.

I was sure I was sabotaging my career if I stayed at my company, but that was okay. I thought, "It's okay if I don't get promoted. Because I let go, I didn't care as much, and I took more risks. I

174

had so much less angst. My family, helping my wife cope with MS, and my daughters, those things were critically important".

At the end of four years I had been promoted twice; I went to director in four years. Someone said to me, "You're the man now, you're the man". I thought, *Whoa!* What a dose of reality! I do need to take what I'm doing seriously. What that meant to me was that I was a living, breathing example of the entire corporation now. How people see you is how they see the company. If you are warm and human, that's what the company is.

I accepted that I was responsible for my life, no one else was.

My big freedom came when I trusted that things could work out. I had to get over this intense fear. The universe forced me into it. I had to recognize I had a choice. I asked myself, on my deathbed, what would I regret? My decisions got really simple and easy. I chose to become part of the solution and make my company the best it could be. I am in charge of my destiny, my wife is doing well, I am proud of my children. What's more— I'm successful in my job because I'm not afraid.

A Blessed Event

This is the story of Ann Fisher's surprise pregnancy upon relocating to Asia, and the roundabout way she became general manager at *Newsweek*, Asia.

In the fall of 1988, Ann was at Ketchum Advertising in San Francisco. An industry veteran with fourteen years under her belt, she was getting itchy for new experiences.

A friend of Ann's knew that she was interested in living overseas, and told her that the Ted Bates agency was looking for someone to work in Jakarta, Indonesia. Ann, not interested in Jakarta but knowing that talking to anyone could be a doorway, took a meeting with the senior executive at Ted Bates who ran the Mars account. After a long conversation in which it was obvious that Indonesia was out, David said there was a regional director job available, a senior role, running the Mars business in Hong Kong.

Ann and Steve flew for a long weekend to Hong Kong. Ann got the job offer and accepted, all in one week. Ann says, "Curiosity drew us, but we had so much naiveté. I was thirty-eight years old, and ready for a change. Steve didn't have a job there yet, but we had a pact: Whoever got the job first, we would go. It was a great opportunity, and Hong Kong was booming. The curiosity trumped the fear".

Two days before Ann got on the plane to go, she found out that she was pregnant. Ann didn't tell anyone except her husband. She'd had a number of miscarriages in the past and wanted to believe this pregnancy would happen.

It wasn't easy. She had morning sickness, she was living in someone else's place until she could find a place to rent and Steve would not be joining her for another month. Every morning, she walked to work, which was directly through the wet market (the meat market).

> I had to tiptoe through the pools of blood, the ox heads, the ducks! I didn't speak any Chinese at that point. It was just overwhelming! The more pregnant I got, the more I wanted American food. I wanted a hamburger and a salad bar, and there just wasn't anything outside of a couple of hotels.

At four months pregnant, Ann told the executives at Bates. Ted Bates was run by two Australian bachelors and a Brit who had been around forever, and it was a twenty-four/seven work culture in a city that never slept. When Ann told her boss, she said, "Two for the price of one". They were not amused.

When they realized however, that Ann was in fact committed to doing a good job they were not as concerned. However, they kept saying, "We can't tell the clients," but soon it would be very obvious! "I was doing store checks in Singapore and Malaysia and I couldn't tell the client I was pregnant. Finally, we told the client, and they were fine. When I first felt my baby move, I was in Taiwan, traveling around."

Ann had three months off unpaid, and took their new daughter to the U.S. for a visit.

> Going back to work was pretty tough; these guys just never stopped working. I would feel guilty because I stopped at 7:00 p.m. and I'd be the first one leaving the office. I had to get really clear about what was right for me, the company, and my family. I did a great job, I focused on my work, I was successful, but I saw that people weren't taking me seriously as a new mom. I decided ultimately that the next year I would leave. Physiologically, my focus was on my child. My brain wasn't clicking the same way the first few months. I took some time to wind down and spend time with her. I thought part-time would be so much better.

After setting the intention to find a new opportunity, Ann met the general manager at *Newsweek*. "My talents and experience fit what they needed, and he said why didn't I apply for the GM at Newsweek—I did, and I got that job in 1990. For me, there's a sense of being open to opportunities. I knew I wanted to work, and I took the opportunity that was there."

With the four practices of Alignment, Ann looked at the reality of the situation. She wanted something new outside of the US and once her daughter was born she wanted a different future. That focus on the future was so important in deciding.

As a duo, Ann and her husband felt like true partners in this, and building that relationship was critical to getting through it. Throughout all of the decision points, they stayed on the same page and supported each other in making their lives what they wanted. They started fresh, they knew practically nobody but, as ex-pats, community was everything, and they did build wonderful friendships in Hong Kong over the eleven years they were there.

In California, Ann had been working on her self-awareness, but in China she began to study different physical and mental practices from all over the world. "Those practices sustained me. It was twice the pace of New York—things that would normally take a week were done in a day, so I needed acupuncture and meditation. I began to do yoga, not on a regular basis, but I was drawn to have something to help me stay grounded."

Ann's final recollection about getting through this wonderful and challenging time?

> I'll also add faith and trust as the way I got through this experience and really enjoyed it. It's not about the absence of fear. It's that fear is trumped by intention, curiosity, yearning, learning, and self-discovery. It's trumped by faith, which comes from experience. I faced adversity as a kid in my family and I learned how to come through no matter what. We had faith in ourselves, in the process, in the idea that if we failed, we would just come back and do something else.

Chapter **10**

When the Worst Does Happen

"Seeing death as the end of life is like seeing the horizon as the end of the ocean."

—*David Searls*

Please note: This section is about the loss of a beloved child and may be disturbing to some readers.

There are moments that are far worse than fear. And it takes Alignment to process those moments. So many of us spend so much time worrying about the worst happening, but when it does, how do we cope? Jay Beckley was working as a senior sales executive at Yahoo! when his five-year-old son, Myles, died in a tragic accident on a family vacation.

I asked Jay about what happens to us when the worst happens, how we survive, what it took for his family to bounce back and to practice Alignment in the face of the unthinkable. This chapter is almost entirely in Jay's words, because they're all that's necessary.

> First of all, Myles was a standout kid. Every parent thinks that about their own kid, but really everyone thought that about Myles. My family was on vacation in Costa Rica, where Myles' mom, Virginia, was born.

Jay, his twelve-year-old daughter, Theresa, and Myles were on horseback on the beach.

> Myles' horse spooked and took off. Myles was hanging on to the reins. Theresa and I immediately got our horses to follow, and we watched him slide down the horse and get dragged over a hundred yards over rocks and through forest. I saw him slip loose and I jumped off my horse, hit the ground, and was surprised at the impact of my feet hitting the ground. I was in

shock. I ran over to Myles lying there, and he was unconscious; he had head injuries he would never recover from. I was in a foreign country. I was afraid, confused, it couldn't be happening. I stayed with Myles; Theresa went back to where her mom was staying. I didn't know what to do, but I knew we needed help. It took us three ambulance rides to get to a hospital. One ambulance broke down. We sat waiting and sweating and praying for another ambulance.

We didn't have cell phones, I didn't speak the language, they didn't speak English. I didn't know how my wife was finding out. Theresa and Virginia beat us to the hospital. Virginia shrieked and crumpled. You couldn't see immediately the trauma, but Virginia knew. It was a crazy scene in the hospital with Virginia talking to the doctors. There was nothing they could do. One doctor, an amazing doctor who cared so much, kept him alive for fifteen minutes until everyone got there, then we had to see him go. We had to say goodbye. Our whole family gathered there: Virginia, Theresa, me, and Casey, who was a year and a half—we were all at the hospital. We started our life over at that moment.

My initial thought was, *'How will we ever recover from this?'* Amazingly, people do. There are examples of people all over the place who survive these things. You don't think in that moment or long after that you can go on. You don't begin to have a formula for it. There's no game plan. Everyone's grief is different. Everyone's tragedy is different.

Something that happened immediately was the amount of love we got from people. Virginia's relatives came from all over. We held each other and prayed. The love, even people who didn't know us—it was overwhelming. People from customs, the morgue, the kind of compassion and love that lives in people was an eye-opener for me. Even in these moments of intense pain, I saw a world I'd never seen before. This was the world I wanted to live in. We had support from community, faith, friends, but it was love that carried us, sustained us, and helped us recover inch by inch.

Sometimes I think, why did someone have to die for this incredible connection to people, for this outpouring of love and positivity to come out?

I got the plane tickets, I drove, I got the hotel—I was the responsible one in those ways. But no one knows what to do. Our family strength was the most important thing. What you can do is to hold each other, and we couldn't let each other shrink away and be alone.

Yahoo! was a model for company compassion. They didn't set out to inspire employees or boost morale, but, boy, did they do that. Anyone who came in contact with that wave of love—it blew all of us away. Why did it take this shocking thing for that company compassion to come out, I don't know, but it did? Some of the things that stood out were immediate. From the top on down throughout the organization, from the CEO to the president to everyone else; they had their priorities right. There was no pressure to work whatsoever. It was about what they could do to help.

There were notes from everyone. An email from the CEO stood out. He said he was sending a virtual hug until he could see me in person. It really hit me when the guy who founded the largest Internet site in the world took time to say that—to reach out.

The guy who ran our Atlanta office helped us with our travel. We ended up coming through Atlanta and had a significant layover. Our guy there had a relationship there with Delta. He made it happen that the flight staff took special care of us on the plane

We were met by a Yahoo! employee at 1:00 a.m. when we finally landed in Detroit; they came to help us get home. When we arrived, dinners started coming from work, emails, calls. Those are just some of the examples. Another thing that was important was that everyone jumped in and covered everything at the office. Other companies could learn a lot—we all have to learn how to deal without someone. I've heard nightmare stories from other parents who've lost children like, "You have three days medical leave". Yahoo! communicated over and over that I had as much time as I needed.

The funeral was twelve days after the accident. We were back in Detroit, in the dead of winter in 2008. The funeral was only two days after we got home from Costa Rica. We had to deal with all the details: programs, pallbearers, readings, arranging the cemetery. The details are inconceivable. Yahoos flew in from all over the country for that funeral.

Other people at Yahoo! responded to the company coming together for us in a powerful way. The message to everyone in the company was that human experience is important. Love is important. Family is important. People fought through their desire not to look at pain this up-close and personal, and they started to talk to me about their own pain, their own humanity. The company focused on the human element. It gave people a sense of commitment and pride in who Yahoo! was. They weren't trying to instill pride or boost morale; they just did the right thing and it had an enormous positive impact.

In a world without real company loyalty, people don't care about a company anymore unless you stand for something. Unless they can find authenticity, caring, learning, and humanity in that company. People know now that products don't bring happiness; experiences do. In that moment, Yahoo! made the decision to live up to something greater than just their business mission—they stood up for paying attention to the human side and it was real and tangible.

Another Yahoo, Mike Murphy, came and said, "I want to do something for Myles". The scholarship fund grew out of that. Mike knows how to do big things, like golf tournaments. I told Mike that we could do a golf tournament if people could play for free. He went out and got Yahoo!, Google, AOL, Facebook, and MSN/ Microsoft to put up the money so we could have people play for free and have money for the scholarship fund.

Our goal is to continue the joy that Myles brought to others. It's not a fundraising organization; it's a joy-raising organization. This is about Myles lighting the world up. We want his picture, his stories, his energy out there.

SMyles Day is a celebration of what's great in our lives. It's a gathering where we put aside our day-to-day and get inspired by Myles and each other. The day is a celebration of a life lived with enough joy and spunk for us all and is designed to create lasting meaning we carry with us. Attendees are truly touched. The SMyles fund provides full scholarships. It also sends an ice-cream truck to the football field each year as a gift of joy. There's so much in people and in our lives that gets covered up with distractions. Let's use Myles to cut through that and have that joy that he did. It's about lighting people up.

When Myles was here, there was no one who didn't fall in love with him. There were seven hundred people at a five-year-old's funeral. They knew him. Someone told me that Myles assumed you loved him, and he loved you. What an amazing kid to impact that many people. He keeps on impacting people.

The Four Practices When the Unthinkable Happens

How can you survive when the worst happens? Remember it's beyond just you. It's a practical thing; people are feeling sorry for themselves; they've lost their job, they lost the football game. Then they see you and they realize they don't have it so bad. It changes their perspective. They watch you go through things and still show up at the market or at the church, and it helps them that you move forward. They're inspired by you when you carry on.

As a family, we've discussed the four practices, and here's what we've come up with.

> *Accepting what is, focusing on the future*—One thing about accepting what is in our particular situation, it makes us remember we're not in control. We may think we're in control, but we're not. We're only in control of how we react to things. It's make or break to recognize that and let that reality be okay. I want to say it's also not just about accepting what is, but in defining what you will accept.
>
> I couldn't have more stark examples of him not being here. I watched the whole experience. But I'm not accepting that he's not here. I have a daily and moment-by-moment battle to keep Myles alive—to believe that he's here now and that we'll be together again. If you're open and awake and willing, those things come all the time. Prayer helps, meditation helps, being connected to things beyond yourself helps.
>
> I feel Myles is with me when I see a butterfly or a rainbow appearing at the right time or a neighbor telling a story about him. Landscapers put in gardens devoted to Myles that we can watch grow. The football program retired number five in his honor. One hundred and fifty football players are wearing jerseys this year that say "Number five is alive in me". Those are being worn all over town. Myles is still here. I went to a basketball game and saw the kids on our home team wearing red wristbands with number five on them. I was so moved. Myles is here. Then I see the other team, and they're all wearing the same red wristband. I had to get a picture of them all together. The swim team planted a tree for Myles. I go to the tree in front of

our house every night to talk to him and connect with him. Yesterday I was at church and I stayed late after mass. A woman said, "Myles' picture is on my fridge, and he gives me joy every day".

Building relationships and community—The impulse for us was to isolate. You don't want to remove the covers from your head. Community is there. They came for us. Myles changed our lives when he came in, when he lived, and he really changed our lives in our relationship and community front when he died.

Tons of people came over during those first weeks. Carol, my sister, was staying here with us and she made the observation that everyone comes to the door, and they say, "This is such a nice house," and it was not the comment itself that struck her; but that it's obvious they've never been here before. Now we are constantly in community. It was not our thing to reach out and go to a pool party or a dinner. If I came home and there was one person in the house that I wasn't expecting it would ruffle my feathers. Now there might be twenty and I'm okay. You can't be alone in tragedy. It's a spiral. You need people. Myles brought those people to us.

Viewing challenges as opportunities—This was a tough one. We can't see opportunity in something so tragic, so devastating. Obviously, all challenges are opportunities. It's the release of Myles' energy from this small container into sharing this joy with thousands of people—that's what sustains us. There is no opportunity that happens from the tragedy, but there is such opportunity in sharing Myles' joy with the world. That's not about his death. It's about Myles, his joy.

Practicing physical and mental discipline—The whole family practices physical and mental discipline, and it is the key to staying grounded. I'm a huge reader and I've always read fiction. From

185

the accident until now I've cracked only one novel. I've been reading spiritual books. I was never a fan of non-fiction, but I was looking for help. It's back to connection and community. I needed to hear the stories of real people. Other families. Other children.

I completed my black belt after Myles died. It was good discipline. It really helped. I coach youth football. We condition our guys a lot. We tell the guys when you're really in shape, it's hard to quit. A lot of going through tragedy and facing change is not quitting. Physical and mental discipline has been important for everyone in my family.

As a family, we did ceremonies together. We go to church a lot. We meditate together. As a family we would sit down with a relative or just by ourselves, and we would go around in a circle and talk about what we were feeling about Myles. We take Theresa to a grief group as a family. Theresa and I hold hands. There were no words, but we knew we were there for each other.

TRY THIS

Cultivating Joy: Live Like Myles

1. Go to www.Myles5.com. Look at pictures, videos, and read some Myles moments. Create pictures and photos of your own. Cherish the time you have with children and the time you spend being joyful and happy.

2. Build a fort in your living space out of blankets and furniture, and have dinner inside.

3. Celebrate children and the joy of play. Schedule playtime. Share it with someone. Everyone needs to play. Kids get it a lot more than we do. Adults need to play.

4. Every time someone wants your attention—your kid, spouse, colleague—give them at least one full-on minute. Take a moment and connect to that person. Say yes and look in their eyes. Focus on them. Give them your attention, even if it's one minute. Myles was so present. Myles expected you loved him. That's where you started your relationship. He was so present. Like any other five-year-old, he was bouncing all over the place. He remembered people's names. He really gave people his attention.

Chapter 11

The Ultimate Goal of Alignment:
The Fourth Circle

"The world has never truly had to develop an ethic of interdependence rooted in our common humanity. And if we do it, the twenty-first century will be the most interesting, exciting, peaceful era in history."

—William Jefferson Clinton

These days, with an eleven-year-old daughter and a community of concerned parents and children during an uncertain time, the most important thing on my mind is the world our child will live in now and when we're gone, and what we're leaving for future generations.

In Nepal, where I adopted my daughter, a quarter of the population live on less than U.S. fifty cents a day. Electricity is in short supply, and the lights are on for about five hours in a twenty-four-hour period, which makes doing business challenging in Kathmandu. Food is scarce and, in 2020, the country has 'severe food insecurity and malnutrition," according to the Zero Hunger Strategic Review. Thirty-six percent of children under five are chronically malnourished.

Nepal, like many poor nations, is on the frontlines of ecological and social un-sustainability. One of the most beautiful places in the world, the birthplace of the Buddha and home of the highest peaks of the Himalayas, it is facing tremendous change, and fast.

Since the first Westerners climbed Everest in 1953, the largest glacier has shrunk over two miles and the Himalayan glaciers are predicted to completely melt by 2035. Rivers like the Ganges, Indus, and Yangtze would slow to a tiny trickle or dry up completely for whole seasons. The results?

—

Food and water shortages, masses of refugees seeking sustenance, and a food crisis for the world, which imports grain from these fertile regions. [24]

Our task now is to remember how truly connected we all are. We should all be concerned about what's happening on Mt. Everest because our collective rice bowls may soon be empty as a result. And there is still time to do something about it.

Inspiring leadership means reminding others that the whole is greater than the sum of its' parts, and we're part of something bigger than ourselves. That reminder gives us a sense of shared responsibility and shared purpose.

If we are not feeling some trepidation when we look at what's happening right now with the effects of global population expansion, climate change, and global poverty, then we are not paying attention. The natural "shut-down" mechanism we've used to block out ugly truths needs to be removed if we're to take fast enough action.

The most useful way to focus on these very real changes, of course? Alignment! Have confidence that you can personally create a more positive outcome. And, together, it can be exponential.

The Fourth Circle

At the center of the circle is you, you have the capacity to have tremendous impact on many levels: on yourself, on those people with whom you immediately interface, on your organization, and on your world as a whole.

The fourth circle is our impact on our greater world. When we are conscious of our interconnection and interdependence with the larger environment around us, we are able to focus on the ultimate goal of individual, team, and organizational Alignment—creating a more just, peaceful, and sustainable world.

---

[24] Tom Owen-Smith. "Climactic Change" *Nepali Times* Issue #393, March, 2008

Looking at the challenges we face, it's no time for shrinking violets! It's time for inspiring leaders to stand up and push for innovation, to champion positive possibilities, and to remain flexible and adaptive during rapid change.

In business thinking, there is a new paradigm beyond the breakthrough systems thinking of the last three decades. That new paradigm is that we are all part of a single, highly complex organism that must function as a whole as well as a series of parts. We need to start looking at the health of our organizations in the context of the health of our entire planetary system.

Without a doubt we are in trouble as a species if we do not change. And there is only one way to change for the positive—to activate our Alignment, to look not at the catastrophe of where we are going with terror, paralysis, fight, or flight, but to look at the future as full of possibility and potential, taking into account the reality of our situation, and moving forward into the future from a positive perspective.

We need to cultivate communities locally, and remember the importance of our relationships to building positive, peaceful coalitions of people who work together rather than at odds. We need to view our enormous challenges as opportunities to start new, better ways of being.

We have started on a new path in business leadership—one that is more ethical, more thoughtful, more integrated into the world community as a whole. MBA students, our future business leaders, have begun to rally around this concept on a grand scale. Started by a small group of Harvard MBAs of the class of 2009, the MBA Oath is a project stewarded by a coalition of MBA students, graduates, and advisors from over two hundred and fifty schools around the globe. They partnered with the Aspen Institute and the World Economic Forum to make a broad impact, and to create a

public conversation about professionalizing and improving management.[25] This is what inspiring leadership looks like. That oath is a powerful declaration of the new direction in which we are headed—and just in the nick of time. The following is a short version from the www.mbaoath.com website.

The MBA Oath

As a manager, my purpose is to serve the greater good by bringing people and resources together to create value that no single individual can create alone. Therefore, I will seek a course that enhances the value my enterprise can create for society over the long term. I recognize my decisions can have far-reaching consequences that affect the well-being of individuals inside and outside my enterprise, today and in the future. As I reconcile the interests of different constituencies, I will face choices that are not easy for me and others.

---

[25] www.mbaoath.com

191

Therefore, I promise:

I will act with utmost integrity and pursue my work in an ethical manner.

I will safeguard the interests of my shareholders, co-workers, customers and the society in which we operate.

I will manage my enterprise in good faith, guarding against decisions and behavior that advance my own narrow ambitions but harm the enterprise and the societies it serves.

I will understand and uphold, both in letter and in spirit, the laws and contracts governing my own conduct and that of my enterprise.

I will take responsibility for my actions, and I will represent the performance and risks of my enterprise accurately and honestly.

I will develop both myself and other managers under my supervision so that the profession continues to grow and contribute to the well-being of society.

I will strive to create sustainable economic, social, and environmental prosperity worldwide.

I will be accountable to my peers and they will be accountable to me for living by this oath.

This oath I make freely, and upon my honor.

People everywhere are declaring their commitments to sustainability and social justice. In 2007, The Designers Accord was a not-for-profit organization founded with the goal of changing the way designers do business. From their website: "The underlying philosophy of this agreement was that by collectively building our intelligence around issues of climate change and humanitarian issues—and tackling those challenges with optimism and creativity— we would catalyze innovative and sustainable problem-solving throughout the creative community".

With adopters in education, corporations, not-for-profits and design firms, this is another fantastic indicator that the will exists. Although it dissolved in 2020, "over half a million designers from around the world participated" in a conversation around "ethics, practices and the responsibilities of the creative community".

Now we need to jump on board to find our place and contribute our gifts, whatever that might look like. It is not the time to say to ourselves, "My contribution will be too small. Who am I to focus on something as big as the whole world or even my whole community?" It's not the time to say, "I don't have time because I'm so responsible for other things: my family, my job, etc". There is no such thing as being too small or too big to contribute what you have to offer to something larger than yourself.

The great news is you're not alone. Not only are MBA students taking a pledge, we are seeing an enormous groundswell of activity for the betterment of our world. Paul Hawken spent over a decade researching organizations dedicated to restoring the environment and fostering social justice. He found over one hundred and thirty thousand of them, and there are more every day.[26] "This movement," says Hawken, "is humanity's immune response...it is about possibilities and solutions. Human kind knows what to do". There are corporate leaders from every sector of business focusing not just on the bottom line, but on new kinds of measures of success, from employee engagement to triple-bottom line reporting. There are leaders at Davos calling for a more ethical capitalism, for greater responsibility, and for new ways of looking at our shared future.

To whom much is given, much is expected, and you, dear reader, have been given a great deal.

---

[26] Paul Hawken. *Blessed Unrest: How the Largest Movement in the World Came Into Being and Why No One Saw it Coming*, Viking Press, NYC, 2007

If you are reading this book, you are a person of privilege. You have the resources, whether your own or someone else's, to have an education, to be able to read, to buy or borrow this book. You have the time to stop focusing on survival, and to start taking time to look at these words on a page or listen to an audiobook. You also have the time to claim your birthright of joy—to start living differently, contributing on a new level to your human family.

The possibilities are incredible and exciting—that you change your working environment for the better, then you help others to become more engaged and proactive, that you fight for what you want and what you believe, that you don't let negative messages crush you—you let them inspire you to action.

No matter what remote and privileged corner of the universe you reside in, you are RIGHT NOW being impacted by that "perfect storm" referred to in Chapter 1:

- Global pandemic

- Economic globalization and interdependence

- Instantaneous communication of information

- Exponentially increasing world population

- Change in climate, weather patterns, and environment

- Rapid destruction of natural resources and ecosystems

- The survival needs of our organizations are not always aligned with our survival needs as a species.

When we come together and look at how we will contribute to the world, we can use the four practices to guide our discussions. How will we use these tried and true steps to act from Alignment?

- Accepting what is, and focusing on the future

194

- Building relationships and community

- Viewing challenges as opportunities

- Practicing physical and mental discipline

We've already seen companies like BWX, Procter & Gamble, Tom's Shoes and more—all companies of different types and sizes, embracing the idea of a new, more sustainable world, and engaging their workforce in something meaningful that can contribute to the greater good.

There is a next step. And that step is to question the very nature of how our systems work. Are our organizations truly sustainable? Is our economic system truly sustainable? Can we continue the way we have been going and expect a positive future outcome?

Here is the truth: Unlimited growth is not possible in a finite system. We can no longer operate as if the system of continuous growth in which we live is sustainable. The outcomes of a growth-focused model are consumption of all available resources and then die-off. Alignment is the only way to ask these questions in a serious and clear way that provides the opportunity for large-scale change on a level we cannot yet imagine.

Hopelessness and helplessness come from the belief that we do not have control or impact on our environment, and it grows when we believe the past to be indicative of future outcomes.

Let go of the past as an indicator of the present and future.

TRY THIS

Challenge Your Core Belief
that the Past Dictates the Future

For many of us, the idea that things are stable and unchanging makes us feel comfortable and safe. The truth is that huge changes happen on a daily basis, and the way things happened yesterday is not an indicator that those are the way things will happen today.

Take a moment to think of a time when your life was instantly changed. It might be something in your life that was difficult or traumatic, like a death or loss. It may be something joyful and amazing, like a birth.

Take a moment to think of something in our world that instantly changed everything for you. It might be the birth of the Internet, it might be a new medicine or technological innovation, it might be the election of a beloved political candidate, or the fall of a wall or barrier.

Now imagine: If those things can happen, other seemingly miraculous innovations, cultural shifts, and personal breakthroughs are all possible. The past does not dictate the future.

Fourth-Circle Thinking

"Don't waste life in doubts and fears; spend yourself on the work before you, well assured that the right performance of this hour's duties will be the best preparation for the hours and ages that will follow it."

—*Ralph Waldo Emerson*

New ways of thinking are happening right now. From TED Talks sharing ideas around the world, to the Social Innovation Camp which brings "together talented software developers and designers with social innovators to build web-based solutions to real social problems".

196

Thea Polancic, inspiring leader and Founder and Chair of the Chicago Chapter of Conscious Capitalism, began her idea as a simple, local resource for business leaders focused on transforming their organizations to better the world. It immediately expanded into a multi-city organization that is supporting leaders in their unique, individual quests.

> It started because I realized that my life was handled. I could see that I was taken care of in so many respects. I would achieve my goals. I had won the game of being a human being. It left me with this question—what is my unique contribution? Why am I here? What can I create that is big enough to be interesting for the rest of my life?

Thea began an inquiry using the question: "What is my unique contribution to the world?"

> I had chosen to not participate in that inquiry until I was hungry for it. I saw that my area of contribution didn't need to be some noble social purpose—it actually had to be something that I'd already been up to my whole life. It had to involve business. It had to be about raising the awareness of powerful people.

> Then, the next step in my inquiry was driven by one of the most simple but transformative questions anyone ever asked me: "What are you measuring? What will you measure in order to know you are making a difference?" I began to look at global measures. I looked at impact. First, I thought, "I have to transform the whole planet" then I arrived at "How do I start locally?" We then got our first group together—it was called the Chicago Transformational Leadership Exchange then—and it then caught on in other cities already.

What Thea noticed is that:

> Leaders keep trying to win the game of self-maximization. Yet the fundamental emotion behind that is despair because it's an

un-winnable game. At the basis of self-maximization is comparison. In that game, we'll always find ourselves alone, struggling for the elusive 'more.' Leaders know in their hearts there will always be someone with a more expensive commode. Engaging in Conscious Capitalism, they get to cross over into a new world, where they've already won. They're cooked; they've won the game of being a human being. NOW WHAT? Why are they here? What is their uniqueness; what unique and special thing do they have to contribute to the world that could be worth it all? What's possible on the other side of that bridge is being in a new state of contribution—one in which they can have multiple points of view. They can let go of their former way of viewing the world and move into a new context.

People spend the majority of their time at work, and they think that their life is about something else. As Thea says, "It's about having someone's work be the place where they fulfill on their commitments in the world. It goes for everyone, not just leaders and founders, but everyone. How do we create organizations that truly live up to that?"

Thea is an example of a leader unleashing the power of business as a lever for social change, and someone who's building momentum and connection across organizations.

Crowdsourcing and Extraordinary Applications

Crowdsourcing is just one more way to tap into our massive numbers, and with small, limited contributions, we're changing the world for the better in large, expansive ways.

Micro-volunteering—donating short amounts of time anywhere, anytime, with much of it being done online—is being delivered to people through apps, dissolving the barriers to volunteering, specifically time and training, so that any one of us can tap into opportunities to contribute.

Apps such as Zooniverse, connect volunteers with professionals to assist with scientific discoveries. It works much like NASA did with its MoonZoo project, which had volunteers help with is crater identification program; thousands of volunteers, each working for a few minutes here and there, accurately classified eighty-eight thousand images in less than one month. The same task would have taken a NASA scientist two years to accomplish.

The Darwin Challenge, created by great, great, grandson of Charles Darwin Chris Darwin, is a 15-year data focused project conducted via App that is shifting our meat consumption one day at a time. The Darwin Challenge objectives? Improving global health, reducing greenhouse gas emissions, stopping the expansion of factory farms, and reducing forest destruction. How will they do that? By inspiring 280 million people to have two meat-free days per week and tracking their meat consumption.

As new, socially oriented businesses pop up, we're starting to see people who've been part of traditional corporations shift out of the old economy and into the new one.

Ending Slave Labor—The Not for Sale Story

Our corporations have been acknowledging the reality. We must eradicate slave labor and it will take our collective effort to do so. Twenty-seven million people are enslaved today around the globe. Inspiring leader Dr. David Batstone is working to change that statistic. He is a Business Professor at the University of San Francisco School of Management and the author of Not For Sale: The Return of the Global Slave Trade—and How We Can Fight It. He is President and Co-Founder of the Not For Sale Campaign, and creator of Free2Work.com. He's an amazing example of someone who took in some disturbing information, faced what was really happening, and chose to do something about it. David Batstone didn't choose the abolitionist path; it found him.

> It found me in my local restaurant in the San Francisco Bay Area, where I live. Every couple of weeks my wife and I went to

this restaurant. We loved the Tandoori chicken and the idlis and the pappadams. And, y'know, it just never struck us as odd that a lot of the kids who were working in the restaurant, washing the dishes or waiting on the tables, teenagers, sixteen, fifteen, changed over a lot. We just assumed that they were extended members of the family who owned the restaurant. So it was a shock to pick up my newspaper, *The Chronicle*, one morning and discover that this restaurant in San Francisco was the center of a human trafficking ring that had brought over five hundred young adolescents into the United States for the purposes of what our Constitution calls involuntary servitude—slavery.

David was curious and wanted to find out what this was all about. Eventually Batsone would be introduced to people like Kim, who at fourteen years old, was brought to the United States to be a house slave for a pastor of a church. For five years he was a house servant in Worcester, a small town in Massachusetts. David Batsone met young Maria in Los Angeles who was forced to sew twelve to fourteen hours a day and then locked in a broom closet in East Los Angeles. He met seven young women from Cameroon who were brought over to be young paid nannies, but then they ended up actually being house slaves in the homes of wealthy American families in the Maryland and Washington, D.C. area.

> "So, the more people I met, I felt that this was something that was in everybody's backyard, right here in the United States. I started to link it back and I found that it was a global problem and these people were being brought here from everywhere."

He went on a six-continent investigation to find out more and his curiosity and research led him to purposeful action. Already a successful writer, entrepreneur, and ethics professor, he was led to use his talents and relationships to begin the Not for Sale Campaign, Free2Work.com, and SlaveryMap.com.

You know, this is not 'here's another global problem you can feel really bad and guilty about,' but do nothing about. We really can fight this and we can make progress. For me the beginning of that realization was a very inspirational woman in Thailand. I call her a modern-day abolitionist. Kunam is an artist, a painter. She would take her empty canvasses, paints and brushes down to the river front where she saw a lot of young street kids sleeping out in the open air, and she asked them to paint their story and these kids started painting nightmares on canvass.

She couldn't believe that young kids, eleven, twelve, could paint these stories and she asked them, "Where did you get these nightmares?" And they told her, you know, "We're not from Thailand. We're from Laos and Cambodia, Myanmar, Burma. We're from as far away as China and Vietnam." "How'd you get here?" "Well, you know, we were kidnapped, many of us. Some of us were sold by our parents. We all ended up in these bars where men from all over the world calling themselves sex tourists would take advantage of us and do things to us that they would get arrested for doing in their home country."

So Kunam was incensed. That night, she ran into a karaoke bar and saw two young boys and a girl sitting there with a male client and she grabbed them and ran out of the restaurant, out of the bar. It's not the most sophisticated intervention strategy and I wouldn't recommend you do that at home, but she just had this righteous rage and wanted to do something about that and—the next night she went to a second bar and found two little girls talking to another male client, a john, and stole them away. So, you know, when I met her, she had twenty-seven kids and no plan.

Not For Sale began when I made a promise to her that I would help her build a home for those twenty-seven kids. Someone had given her a piece of property in the very far north of Thailand, near the border of Laos, which is an area we call the Golden Triangle. But she had no housing. They were living in lean-to sheds and tents. I made a promise I would raise funds. For those people who read my book, I would ask them for a donation towards a house for Kunam. Well, as I'm writing the book, I keep getting calls from her that, you know, it's not twenty-seven kids; it's now fifty-three. And then she calls another couple weeks later—it's now eighty-seven kids. Wow, one hundred and twenty-seven later, I'm not building a house—I'm building a village for these kids that she's rescued.

And so, today, we have in the Golden Triangle region, a village called Buddies Along the Roadside, where these kids are going to school. And we're now moving towards helping kids not only in Thailand, but all over the world. We founded Not for Sale.

David and his crew visited multiple companies and said they wanted to give them an opportunity to look good; they could make a pledge for their company to be a slavery free company? At Bloomberg financial news, Mayor Bloomberg's finance company had a cover story that revealed that the pig iron that goes into Ford, GM and Toyota cars was being extracted by slaves in Brazil.

David says, "I met a Toyota executive who said, 'I had no idea. Are you sure?' I said, "Well, I'm sure you're not going around the globe saying, 'Hey, where can I find some slave pig iron?' It's more a matter of just finding the cheapest pig iron you can find". Examination of the supply chain is necessary to locate potential areas for improvement.

We haven't had any kind of monitoring. There's no responsibility anywhere along the supply chain. But we want you to look good.

We'll help you educate your supply chain. We'll help you monitor it because you don't want the front page of the New York Times in about a year from now, when this is a growing concern, to say, you know, Ford, the slave company... Executives are keen to do this; those that have a good conscience and then those who fear the reputational damage.

A part of it is simply our ignorance about our global links. We are connected to a global economy. I was walking through an airport and I looked up and I saw a Forbes Magazine and the cover said 'Child Slavery, why we are so addicted.' I picked up the magazine; I was really shocked this was coming from Forbes, a mainstream executive business magazine for American corporations. It's going to take a generation of us to say, no, I don't want to wear someone's suffering. I don't want to eat someone's suffering. And there's very practical things we can do about that.

We need to live and work differently, buy differently. Start with chocolate, then continue shopping with awareness; none of us wants to buy slave-made products. Have better, higher expectations, so that if you see something that could raise a red flag, like David Batstone did in his local Indian restaurant, you can recognize and address it. When we have more transparency and awareness, and shine a light on the hidden corners, it makes a profound difference.

The Power of Simple Conversation

We cannot forget the amazing power of just talking. If we keep spending all of our time running around like the proverbial chicken without its head, we will never use our energy to talk, to debate, and to learn from each other and create together. In most of the companies I work in, I see the value of short meetings, of more streamlined communication. What I don't see is the necessary space and openness for dialog that meanders, explores, challenges our beliefs, and leads us to new ideas. The most exciting thing we can do in this age of instant communication is to take the time to have a long conversation. If you only have time to try one activity in this book, this is the one to try. Make it work for you. Explore and enjoy.

TRY THIS
Provocative Conversations

Step One: Find a group of eight or fewer curious, interesting colleagues and make a commitment to a three-month series of conversations about something you find compelling and challenging in your business—something that doesn't immediately seem solvable or easy, but that you all feel curious or passionate about.

Step Two: Start a discussion using a provocative idea. You may want to use an outside facilitator, or elect someone in your group with excellent facilitation skills. I highly suggest that food and beverages be present and this be framed as an enjoyable exploration…even if it's conducted virtually.

Step Three: Let your conversation wander. Explore. Take time to separate and do research, to find things out and report back to your small group.

Step Four: Before your last meeting, each contributor can come up with a series of ideas for action. These proposed ideas must be ideas that can be acted upon by the members of the group. It could mean making a proposal to someone in the organization or it could be direct action.

Step Five: At your last session, commit to the actions the group is willing to take. Each person must commit to at least one action item. Come back together in another month to see how it went!

Sample provocative propositions using the word "AND":

How might we build our business AND replenish all the natural resources we're using?

How can we build a culture of productivity AND help people spend more time with their families and in their communities?

How can we ensure our supply chain is free of slave labor AND ensure we are resourcing the least-expensive materials?

What would need to be in place in order to be profitable AND ecologically sustainable?

How can we add vibrancy and meaning into our workplace AND stay focused?

A Dream We Can Share

A world in which businesses large and small are fulfilling their purpose in ways that are generative for their customers, their employees, their owners, and their environment— this is a world in which our children's great-great-grandchildren have plentiful food, clean water, places to play, and communities full of connection, collaboration, and shared experiences of joy.

It is a world in which we spend less time in fear, and more time in creative expression, service to others, and where we feel lucky to be alive.

This is a world that is accessible to all of us.

What are we waiting for?

Appendix

Things You Can Do

If *Inspiring Leadership in Uncertain Times* inspires you, here are some suggestions for building momentum with these ideas:

1. The most important step? Really do the exercises! Don't just read them—practice, and you'll reap the benefits.

2. Visit www.karlinsloan.com or www.sloangroupinternational.com for more information on programs based on this book, including workshops, webinars, lectures, and custom programs for organizational leaders and their teams.

3. Invite Karlin Sloan to speak at your company or professional association by inquiring at community@sloanleaders.com.

4. Suggest *Inspiring Leadership in Uncertain Times* to a friend or colleague, to your team or workgroup, to your management class or leadership body.

5. Create a reading group to discuss the principles of the book, and work with each other to support your process in working the exercises.

6. Write a book review in a newsletter, on a blog, or on Amazon.com; this always helps promote the books you enjoy!

7. Become a Member of **Inspiring Leadership** by downloading the app for Android or iOS. Make a commitment to yourself and to your world to do something that gives back, makes life better, creates joy, and expands the positive. Submit that pledge to a supportive community of like-minded leaders at www.InspiringLeadership.io and participate in a year long journey to become a more Inspiring Leader.

About the Author

Karlin Sloan is an author, speaker, and leadership consultant who believes that business leaders have a responsibility not just to make their organizations better, but to contribute to the world in a positive way. As the Founder and CEO of Sloan Group International Ms. Sloan provides leadership and management development consulting, training and executive coaching to clients in the U.S., Europe, South America, Asia, Australia and New Zealand. She has helped organizations to develop clearer, more effective communication, enhanced teamwork and powerful leadership in times of growth, challenge, and change.

Bibliography

Alexander, C. *The Endurance: Shackleton's Legendary Antarctic Expedition*. Knopf, 1998

Argyle, M. *The Psychology of Happiness*. Routledge, 2001

Bemporad, R. and M. Baranowski. *Conscious Consumers Are Changing the Rules of Marketing. Are You Ready?* Whitepaper, November 2007

Benard, B. *Resiliency: What We Have Learned*. San Francisco: WestEd, 2004

Brahm, A. *Mindfulness, Bliss, and Beyond: A Meditator's Handbook*. Wisdom Publications, 2005

Cameron, J. *The Artist's Way*, Tarcher, 1992

Cannon, WB. *Bodily Changes in Pain, Hunger, Fear and Rage: An Account of*

Recent Research Into the Function of Emotional Excitement, 2nd ed. New York, Appleton-Century-Crofts, 1929

Charan, R. *Leadership in the Era of Economic Uncertainty*. McGraw Hill, 2009

Church, F. *Freedom from Fear*. NY: St. Martins Press, 2004

Collins, J. and Porras, J. *Built to Last*. Harper Paperbacks; 3 edition, 2002

Csikszentmihalyi, M. *Flow: The Psychology of Optimal Experience*. HarperCollins Publishers, 1990

Fredrickson, B. L. "The Value of Positive Emotions." *American Scientist* 91, 330-335, 2003

Gunaratana, B.H. *Mindfulness in Plain English*. Wisdom Publications, 2002

Haidt, J. *The Happiness Hypothesis*. Basic Books, 2005

Haidt, J. "Elevation and the positive psychology of morality." In C. L. M.

Keyes and J. Haidt (eds.) *Flourishing: Positive Psychology and the Life Well-lived.* Washington, D.C.: American Psychological Association, 2003, pp. 275-289

Hanh, T.N. *The Miracle of Mindfulness: A Manual on Meditation.* Beacon Press, 1996

Hawken, P. *Blessed Unrest: How the Largest Movement in the World Came Into Being and Why No One Saw it Coming.* Viking Press, NYC, 2007

Holling, C.S., L. Gunderson, and G. Peterson. "Sustainability and Panarchies" in *Panarchy: Understanding Transformations in Human and Natural Systems.* L.H. Gunderson and C.S. Holling (eds). Island Press, Washington, D.C., 2002, pp. 63-102

Holling, C.S., L. Gunderson, and D. Ludwig. "In Quest of a Theory of Adaptive Change" in *Panarchy: Understanding Transformations in Human and Natural Systems.* L.H. Gunderson and C.S. Holling (eds). Island Press, Washington, D.C., 2002, pp. 3-24

Kabat-Zinn, J. *Full Catastrophe Living: How to Cope with Stress, Pain and Illness Using Mindfulness Meditation.* London: Piatkus. 1996

Kahneman, D.D. ed., Schwarz, Norbert. *Well-Being: The Foundations of Hedonic Psychology.* Russell Sage Foundation Publications, 2003

Keyes and J. Haidt (eds.) *Flourishing: Positive Psychology and the Life Well-lived.* Washington, D.C.: American Psychological Association, 2003, pp. 275-289

Maslow, A.H. "A Theory of Human Motivation." *Psychological Review* 50(4) 370-96. 1943

Marks, I. M. *Fears, Phobias and Rituals: Panic, Anxiety, and their Disorders.* Oxford: Oxford University Press. 1987

McMahon, D.M. *Happiness: A History.* Atlantic Monthly Press, 2006

Owen-Smith, T. "Climactic Change" *Nepali Times* Issue #393, March, 2008

Robbins, B.D. "What is the good life? Positive psychology and the renaissance of humanistic psychology." *The Humanistic Psychologist*, 36(2), 2008, pp. 96-112

Rosenman, S. (ed). *The Public Papers of Franklin D. Roosevelt, Volume Two: The Year of Crisis, 1933.* New York: Random House. 11–16. 1938

Rozell, N. "St. Matthew Island--Overshoot and Collapse," *Alaska Science*,November 23, 2003

Seligman, M. *Learned Optimism: How to Change Your Mind and Your Life.* Free Press, 1990

Shenk, J.W. "What Makes Us Happy?" *The Atlantic.* July 2009

Werner, E.E. and R.S. Smith. *Overcoming the Odds: High Risk Children from Birth to Adulthood.* Ithaca, NY: Cornell University Press, 1992

Werner, E.E. and R.S. Smith. *Vulnerable but Invincible: A Longitudinal Study of Resilient Children and Youth.* New York: McGraw Hill, 1982

Vaillant, G. *Aging Well: Surprising Guideposts to a Happier Life from the Landmark Harvard Study of Adult Development.* New York: Little Brown, 2003

Weiss, A. *Beginning Mindfulness: Learning the Way of Awareness.* New World Library, 2004

Wheatley, M. *Finding our Way.* San Francisco: Berrett Koehler, 2005

Wolins, S., and S. Wolins. *The Resilient Self: How Survivors of Troubled Families Rise Above Adversity.* Villard, 1993

9 781087 860770